"The good news of Christm.␣␣␣␣␣␣␣␣␣␣␣␣␣␣␣␣␣␣␣␣␣␣.ıth the Christmas story. *The One True*␣␣␣␣␣␣␣␣␣␣␣␣.ıe narratives and themes of the Old Testament finc␣␣␣␣␣␣.ıt in the coming of Christ. Tim Chester peels away the layers of familiarity that hinder us from seeing the babe of Bethlehem in all his glory. Are you longing to focus on something other than all you need to do and buy before Christmas? This book will draw you into the gospel story and help set your heart on Christ during this Advent season."

Betsy Childs Howard,

Author, blogger and editor for The Gospel Coalition

"Every year our Advent candle builds expectation for Christmas, but it burns down to nothing. This wonderful book will create expectation and leave you feeling moved, joyful, thankful and awestruck. You will not be empty-handed or empty-hearted after spending a month with these devotions. Along the way, you will learn to see the riches of Christ in the Old Testament and feel a fresh impetus to see the centrality of the story of Jesus in the pages of your Bible."

Adrian Reynolds,

Director of Ministry, The Proclamation Trust

"Have you become a Christmas cynic like me, jaded by a commercialised holiday? Instead of saying 'bah humbug,' let Tim Chester take you past the trees and tinsel to the ancient biblical drama that led up to Jesus' birth. *The One True Story* connects the familiar Christmas story to God's mighty works in the past, as well as to our lives in the modern world, with freshness and delight."

Jeramie Rinne,

Senior Pastor, Evangelical Community Church of Abu Dhabi

Tim Chester

The One True Story

Daily readings for Advent
from Genesis to Jesus

thegoodbook
COMPANY

The One True Story

© Tim Chester/The Good Book Company, 2016. Reprinted 2016, 2017.

Published by
The Good Book Company
Tel (UK): 0333 123 0880
International: +44 (0) 208 942 0880
Email: info@thegoodbook.co.uk

Websites:
UK: www.thegoodbook.co.uk
North America: www.thegoodbook.com
Australia: www.thegoodbook.com.au
New Zealand: www.thegoodbook.co.nz

Unless indicated, all Scripture references are taken from the HOLY BIBLE,
NEW INTERNATIONAL VERSION. Copyright © 2011 Biblica, Inc.™
Used by permission.

ISBN: 9781784981532

Design by André Parker

Printed in India

Contents

Introduction
The One True Story

Everyone loves the Christmas story—Mary meeting an angel, being told she's having a baby by the Holy Spirit, Joseph faithfully standing by her, travelling to Bethlehem while Mary is heavily pregnant, no room at the inn, the baby in a manger, God in human flesh, choirs of angels, shepherds on the hillside, Magi following a star.

But the Christmas story is not just a great story. It's *the* great story. It's the story that ties together a thousand other stories. Everything came together on that night in Bethlehem. "The fulfilment of the ages," Paul calls it.

Matthew can't get the old stories out of his head as he tells the Christmas story. Five times he says that what happened at the birth of Jesus took place to fulfil what the prophets had said (Matthew 1 v 22-23; 2 v 5-6, 15, 17-18, 23). Luke makes the same point in the four songs he records. The songs of Mary, Zechariah, the angels and Simeon all riff on "tunes" from the past. Mary ends her song with the words, "He has helped his servant Israel, remembering to be merciful to Abraham and his descendants for ever, just as he promised our ancestors" (Luke 1 v 54-55). As the carol *O Little Town of Bethlehem* says, "The hopes and fears of all the years are met in thee tonight".

The Christmas story is the one true story because it completes and fulfils *all* the stories of the Bible.

But it also *goes on* being the one true story. This is the story that makes sense of my story and your story. We were made to know God. All our longings only truly find their fulfilment in him and through him. The plotlines of our lives are meant to find their resolution in the enjoyment of God. But we've set our lives on other trajectories which always lead to disappointing endings.

But through the Christmas story God is rewriting the story of human history, bringing it to a glorious climax. In all the busyness of Christmas, don't miss the opportunity to discover or rediscover how you can be part of the one true story.

~

Each day we'll look at one or two stories from the Bible to see how they find their fulfilment in the Christmas story and to explore how the Christmas story connects with our stories. I've identified the storyline for each chapter. Do try to read the Bible passages for yourself. But don't worry if you don't have time to read any or all of them, as each story is summarised as we go along.

Each chapter ends with a meditation and a prayer. Where no source is given, I've written them myself.

~

The firstborn

*"The Son is the image of the invisible God,
the firstborn over all creation."*
Colossians 1 v 15

Storyline
Proverbs 8 v 22-31 and Colossians 1 v 15-20

What is it about small babies that makes us go gooey? They're not very useful. In fact there's almost nothing they can do except wail and poop. And, to be honest, they're not always that pretty. Most of them look like a miniature version of Winston Churchill.

Yet when we hold them in our arms, our hearts melt. And when they smile, even the hardened cynic is won over.

The evolutionary biologists tell us this is about the instinct to preserve our genes. Perhaps. But we have similar feelings about other people's children. Indeed, we go a bit gooey about chicks, puppies, kittens, lambs, calves and foals. There's something about the newness of life that captures our hearts.

Perhaps that's one reason why we love the Christmas story.

But Christmas is not the *beginning* of the story of the baby in the manger. The baby in the manger was old and new and always new. When Paul writes to the Colossians, he includes a hymn about Jesus. It begins:

The Son is the image of the invisible God,
the firstborn over all creation.   Colossians 1 v 15

Jesus was born into our world on the first Christmas Day. Thousands of people had already been born before that date. But Jesus is the "firstborn" because he existed before any of them. Abraham was born at least 2,000 years before Jesus. But Jesus said, "Before Abraham was born, I am" (John 8 v 58). His birth into this world came *after* Abraham's birth. But his existence came long *before* Abraham. Indeed so long before that it has no date. That's not just because it was in some forgotten pre-history. It's because Jesus has *always* existed. He doesn't say, *I was born before Abraham was born.* He says, "Before Abraham was born, I am". I AM was how God described his external existence to Moses from the burning bush in Exodus 3. And Jesus is God: he is one of the three Persons of the triune God.

From the earliest times the church has said that Jesus is "eternally begotten". He wasn't born in the sense that there was time before he existed and then he was born into existence. No, he has eternally been given life from God the Father. It's a tough idea for us to get our heads round. Jesus himself says, "For as the Father has life in himself, so he has granted the Son also to have life in himself" (John 5 v 26).

The early church fathers described the Father as the fountainhead of the triune God. Imagine an eternal fountain, eternally pouring out clear, clean water. Around it is an eternal pool. The pool receives its water from the fountain. But, because the fountain is eternal, the pool is also eternal. Although it depends on the fountain for its water, there was never a time when it didn't exist. In the same way the Son receives life from the Father—and in that sense is begotten.

But there was never a time when the Son did not exist—and so he is eternally begotten.

This eternal begetting means the life of the Son is always new. He never grows old. There is always a freshness to his life. And he is full of joy.

∽

Children love doing the same thing over and over again. My two-year-old friend Tayden loves it when I throw him over my shoulder, and dangle him down my back with one hand while I reach round with the other hand so I can scoop him round, flipping him over in the process, to land him on his feet by my side. *"Again!"* he cries. *"Again!" "Again!"*

His capacity to do it again always exceeds mine. His joy is undiminished by repetition. It's as if it's always new for him. Children have a delight in the world because to them it's new. Too often the rest of us have grown old and weary of the simple joys of life.

But the life of Jesus is *always new.* And the joy of Jesus is always fresh. Proverbs 8 personifies Wisdom and celebrates its role in creation. The New Testament suggests Jesus is that Wisdom. And in Proverbs 8 v 30-31 Wisdom-Jesus says:

> *Then I was constantly at his side.*
> *I was filled with delight day after day,*
> *rejoicing always in his presence,*
> *rejoicing in his whole world*
> *and delighting in the human race.*

"Delighting day after day." "Rejoicing always."

∽

But the Jesus born in the manger was not "rejoicing always". Sometimes he wept; sometimes he was angry. That's because death had entered the world because of human rebellion. So now the world is subject to decay. There's still plenty to bring delight. But there's also sorrow and pain. Christmas can be a time when we're reminded of a lost loved one or a time when family conflict reaches fever pitch.

The good news is that the hymn in Colossians goes on. Not only is Jesus the firstborn over creation; he's also the firstborn over a *new creation*. Colossians 1 v 18 says Jesus…

is the beginning and the firstborn from among the dead.

Jesus died bearing the penalty of our sin. But at his resurrection he was, as it were, reborn—the beginning and promise of a world made new. At Christmas the story of creation starts a new chapter. It becomes the story of re-creation.

Jesus said, "I have come that [you] might have life, and have it to the full" (John 10 v 10). The life that flows from the Father to the Son flows to us through the death of the Son. That means we can look forward to eternal life instead of eternal death. But it also means new life. "If anyone is in Christ," says 2 Corinthians 5 v 17, "the new creation has come: the old has gone, the new is here!" One day we will be people made new in a world made new. But even now we have life. And that includes a new perspective on the world. We see the world as a gift from God.

It's not hard to be a curmudgeon at Christmas: the same old decorations, the same old routines, the same old television programmes, the same old family arguments. This Christmas try to rediscover the joy of simple things. Try to see the world through the eyes of a child. Try to look at the world filled with the wonder and newness of God's Son and cry, *"Again!"*

～

Meditate

*"The Son is the image of the invisible God,
the firstborn over all creation."*

*Lo, within a manger lies
He who built the starry skies …
Sacred Infant, all divine,
What a tender love was thine,
Thus to come from highest bliss
Down to such a world as this.*

(From "See, amid the winter's snow" by Edward Caswall)

～

Prayer

*For the beauty of the earth,
for the beauty of the skies,
for the Love which from our birth
over and around us lies:
Christ, our God, to thee we raise
this our Sacrifice of Praise.
Amen.*

(From "For the beauty of the earth" by Folliott S. Pierpoint)

The new  Adam

"But we do see Jesus, who was made lower than the angels for a little while, now crowned with glory and honour because he suffered death, so that by the grace of God he might taste death for everyone."

Hebrews 2 v 9

Storyline

Genesis 1 v 26 – 2 v 7; Psalm 8 and Hebrews 2 v 5-18

Someone has decided to destroy the earth to make way for an intergalactic bypass. And they forget to tell us. That's how Douglas Adams' comic classic *The Hitch-Hiker's Guide to the Galaxy* begins. It's Adams' way of highlighting how insignificant our small planet is compared to the vastness of the universe.

Marvel #1. Three thousand years ago King David looked up at the stars and come to much the same conclusions.

When I consider your heavens, the work of your fingers,
the moon and the stars,
   which you have set in place,
what is mankind that you are mindful of them,
human beings that you care for them?　　　Psalm 8 v 3-4

We are small-part players on an insignificant planet orbiting a small star in an insignificant part of the universe.

Marvel #2. But David says the bigger marvel is this:

> *You have made them a little lower than the angels*
> *and crowned them with glory and honour.*
> *You made them rulers over the works of your hands;*
> *you put everything under their feet.*   Psalm 8 v 5-6

The bigger marvel is that God has honoured humanity in an extraordinary way. We're up there with the angels. Some modern Bible translations use the words "them ... them ... them ... their" because the psalmist is talking about human beings. But it's literally "him ... him ... him ... his." That's because the psalmist is speaking of the first man, Adam, as the representative of humanity.

On the sixth day of creation God made Adam. The word "adam" means "humanity". The first man was the beginning and representative of all humanity. God formed him from the dust, creating a mannequin of inert clay. And then God breathed his "breath" or "Spirit" into the clay so that Adam became a living being. And God placed all things under his authority and care.

Marvel #3 is the reality check. The writer of Hebrews meditates on Psalm 8. But his conclusion is, "At present we do not see everything subject to him" (Hebrews 2 v 8, see NIV footnote). Something went badly wrong. The world is not under our control. Last Christmas the river in our town burst its banks. A number of houses were flooded. The bridge was closed. Groups of people walked around to marvel at the power of nature. For all our technological advances, this world is not under our control.

What went wrong was Adam's rebellion against God. Adam sinned against God and that sin brought death and judgment into the world. The ground was cursed and our relationship with the world around us became a struggle. Sometimes we exploit the planet. Sometimes the natural world turns on us.

Marvel #4. At the first Christmas a second Adam was born into the world. At Christmas the story of humanity was replayed, but this time with a different outcome. The central act first time round was disobedience and the outcome was conflict and judgment. The central act second time round was obedience and the outcome is victory and peace. Reworking the language of Psalm 2, Hebrews 2 v 8-9 continues:

> *At present we do not see everything subject to them. But we do see Jesus, who was made lower than the angels for a little while, now crowned with glory and honour because he suffered death, so that by the grace of God he might taste death for everyone.*

Jesus is the Son of God, "as much superior to the angels as the name he has inherited is superior to theirs" (Hebrews 1 v 4). But at the first Christmas he was made lower than the angels. He became human, lived on earth, suffered what we suffer. He was hungry, thirsty, tired. He was rejected, abused, betrayed. Hebrews 2 v 10 says he was made "perfect through what he suffered". That doesn't mean he had a fault that needed straightening out. It means he became perfectly equipped to save us. He fully experienced what it is to be human. "Since the children have flesh and blood, he too shared in their humanity" (Hebrews 2 v 14). Jesus wasn't playing at being human. He wasn't like an actor who can step out of his part at the end of the performance. Jesus is fully, truly, perfectly human. He is the new and true Adam.

∾

So what?

First, Jesus subdues our world. Everything has been placed under his feet. He reigns now in heaven and one day he'll reign on earth. Jesus is the true Adam through whom our humanity is restored and through whom our care over the world will be restored.

Second, he shares our pain.

> *For this reason he had to be made like them, fully human in every way, in order that he might become a merciful and faithful high priest in service to God, and that he might make atonement for the sins of the people. Because he himself suffered when he was tempted, he is able to help those who are being tempted.*
>
> Hebrews 2 v 17-18

Are you suffering? Jesus knows what it is to suffer. Are you tempted? Jesus knows what it is to be tempted. And he is a merciful high priest. He's not saying, *You have no idea what it is to suffer—if you only knew how much I suffered.* Quite the opposite. He's saying, *I have an idea what it's like for you—I know how much you're suffering.* Or maybe you're weighed down by guilt. Know this for certain today—Jesus makes atonement for your sin.

As we prepare to celebrate the birth of the new, true Adam, we can confidently rejoice in sins forgiven now, and the renewal of everything in the new creation.

∽

Meditate

"But we do see Jesus, who was made lower than the angels for a little while, now crowned with glory and honour because he suffered death, so that by the grace of God he might taste death for everyone."

O loving wisdom of our God!
When all was sin and shame,
A second Adam to the fight
And to the rescue came.

O wisest love, that flesh and blood,
Which did in Adam fail,
Should strive afresh against the foe,
Should strive and should prevail.

(From "Praise to the Holiest in the height" by John Henry Newman)

~

Prayer

Now display thy saving pow'r,
Ruin'd nature now restore;
Now in mystic union join
Thine to ours, and ours to thine.

Adam's Likeness, Lord, efface,
Stamp thy Image in its place.
Second Adam from above,
Reinstate us in thy love.
Amen.

(From "Hark, the herald angels sing" by Charles Wesley)

The dragon-slayer

"She gave birth to a son, a male child …
The great dragon was hurled down—that ancient snake
called the devil, or Satan, who leads the whole world astray."
Revelation 12 v 5, 9

Storyline
Genesis 3 v 1-15 and Revelation 12

We're all familiar with the historical version of the Christmas story—the angelic messengers, the journey to Bethlehem, the child in the manger, the visit of the shepherds and so on. This is the version told in the Gospels.

But there is another version of the story—a mythological one. This is the version told by John in the book of Revelation. By "mythological" I don't mean untrue, though it's certainly very different from the historical versions in the Gospels. This version is rich with symbolism. John speaks of "signs". Instead of the story from a historical perspective, this is the story from an eternal perspective.

‿

But before we get there, we need to go back to Adam and Eve in the garden. The serpent, we're told, came to Eve, inviting her to question God's word and reject God's authority. At this point Adam should have stepped in. God had told him to protect the garden. He should have stamped on the serpent and that would have been that. But Adam was strangely silent. Culpably silent. As a result Adam and Eve disobeyed God and were exiled from God's presence in the garden. And that might have been that. But God gave a warning to the serpent which was really a promise to humanity—the promise of a serpent-crusher:

> *I will put enmity*
> *between you and the woman,*
> *and between your offspring and hers;*
> *he will crush your head,*
> *and you will strike his heel.*   Genesis 3 v 15

This is the background to John's mythological version of the Christmas story in Revelation 12.

∽

John sees a woman in heaven clothed with the sun, with the moon under her feet and a crown of stars on her head. At the same time he sees an enormous red dragon with seven heads and ten horns. Its tail sweeps a third of the stars from the sky. The woman is pregnant and the dragon stands poised to catch her child the moment he is born. But at the last minute the child is snatched up to God. War breaks out in heaven between Michael (God's chief angel) and the dragon. Eventually Michael overpowers the dragon, who is thrown down to the earth. Meanwhile the women escapes into the wilderness. The dragon pursues her, but she's given two eagle-wings to fly out of his reach. The dragon spews a great flood of water out of his mouth to overwhelm her. But the ground opens up to swallow it and she escapes. So the dragon is left furiously waging war against the offspring of the women.

Not the version of the Christmas story you get on Christmas cards! Both Matthew's and John's accounts have the words, "She gave birth to a son" (Matthew 1 v 25; Revelation 12 v 5). But not much else is the same.

Fortunately, John decodes enough of the story for us to get the point. The dragon, he says, is "that ancient snake called the devil, or Satan, who leads the whole world astray" (v 8). The dragon in the story is the serpent in the garden. The woman represents God's people and her child is Jesus. God promised the serpent-crusher would come from the family of Abraham and the nation of Israel, his people in the Old Testament. And so it was. God's people (in the person of Mary) gave birth to Jesus. Here are the events of Christmas Day played out on the stage of history and eternity.

But the story is not yet over. It seemed that Satan was going to crush Jesus at the cross. In fact he only bruised his heel, as it were. For God raised Jesus from the dead and Jesus ascended to heaven. "The child was snatched up to God and to his throne," says John (v 7). The battle in heaven is the fruit of the battle that took place on earth at the cross. The bruising of Jesus turns out to be the crushing of Satan. So Satan turns his attention on God's people, the church. And he would have destroyed the church long ago if God were not protecting it. John pictures this protection as the gift of eagle's wings and the ground swallowing up Satan's flood of water. The church itself is safe, though many of her members (her "children") are cruelly persecuted.

It's all a bit breathless. The scale of this story is vast and the pace is relentless. You might want to take a moment to let it sink in. John wants to capture our imaginations. He wants us to see our lives on the stage of history and eternity. We, too, feel:

- the **seductions** of the serpent as he encourages us to question God's word and reject God's rule.
- the **accusations** of the serpent as he points to our sin and encourages us to doubt God's grace (v 10).
- the **threats** of the serpent as he wages war against the church.

But the message of John's epic version of the Christmas story is this:

> *They triumphed over him*
> *by the blood of the Lamb*
> *and by the word of their testimony;*
> *they did not love their lives so much*
> *as to shrink from death.*   v 11

What do we do when temptation comes our way and Satan portrays God's rule as restrictive? We look in the manger and see God's generosity.

What do we do when we sin and Satan accuses us? We look in the manger and see God's rescue mission for sinners.

What do we do when we're under pressure as Christians? We look in the manger and see the serpent-crusher.

And we look from the manger to the cross, and from the cross to heaven, where Christ already reigns. For we have overcome through the blood of the Lamb. And then we testify. We proclaim the victory of Christ's blood. For we overcome through the word of our testimony.

You may not feel that you are particularly under threat at the moment. But there are many others in your church, in this country, and around the world who feel the fiery breath of the dragon on their necks today. In fact, Christmas is a time of *increased* danger for some Christians. So in the midst of the festive rush, why not take some time to pray for our persecuted brothers and sisters throughout the world who feel the rage of the ancient enemy most today (v 17)?

Meditate

She gave birth to a son, a male child ...
The great dragon was hurled down—that ancient snake called
the devil, or Satan, who leads the whole world astray.

Faith, see the place, and see the tree
Where heaven's Prince, instead of me,
Was nailed to bear my shame.
Bruised was the dragon by the Son,
Though two had wounds, there conquered One –
And Jesus was his name.

(From "In Eden—sad indeed that day"
by William Williams, translated by R. M. Jones)

∾

Prayer

God of love, whose compassion never fails;
we bring before thee
the troubles and perils of people and nations,
the sighing of prisoners and captives,
the sorrows of the bereaved,
the necessities of strangers,
the helplessness of the weak,
the despondency of the weary,
the failing powers of the aged.
O Lord, draw near to each;
for the sake of Jesus Christ our Lord.

(Anselm of Canterbury)

The true brother

"You have come ... to Jesus the mediator of a new covenant, and to the sprinkled blood that speaks a better word than the blood of Abel."
Hebrews 12 v 22, 24

Storyline
Genesis 4

"Listen! Your brother's blood cries out to me from the ground." So says God in Genesis 4 v 10. *Can you hear it? Can you hear the blood of Abel?*

~

Eve, the first woman, gave birth to two sons, Cain and Abel (Genesis 4 v 1). Both brought an offering to God. Right at the beginning of the human story, people were aware that our sin needs to be atoned for. In other words, something needs to be done to put things right—and that something involves sacrifice.

Cain worked the soil and so he brought an offering from his crops. Abel kept flocks and offered some animals. God looked with favour on Abel's offering, but not on Cain's. We're not told why. But perhaps there's a clue in the description of Abel's offering. He gave "fat portions from some of the firstborn of his flock" (v 4). This was the best of the best. And perhaps that reflects the heart which made the offering.

But it threw Cain into a big sulk. He "was very angry, and his face was downcast" (v 5). So God graciously spoke to him with both a promise and a warning.

- ᴇ **The promise:** "If you do what is right, will you not be accepted?"
- ᴇ **The warning:** "Sin is crouching at your door; it desires to have you, but you must rule over it." (v 7)

How, I wonder, is sin crouching at your door? Are you ready to fight it? Cain wasn't. He lured Abel out into the field and murdered him in cold blood.

God came to Cain a second time: "Where is your brother Abel?" Cain famously responded: "I don't know … Am I my brother's keeper?" (v 9) But Cain did know and so did God. "Listen!" says God. "Your brother's blood cries out to me from the ground" (v 10).

In Genesis 3 Adam and Eve were sent east from the Garden of Eden, east from God's presence. Now in Genesis 4, "Cain went out from the LORD's presence and live in the land of Nod, east of Eden" (v 16). Cain was further east, condemned to live as a wanderer in exile from God's presence.

∽

"Listen!" It's a very powerful moment.

Cain thinks his crime has gone unseen and unheard—after all, he lured Abel out into a field. But Abel's blood has become audible. It cries out for justice. And not just Abel's blood. The blood of all the oppressed of humanity cries out for justice. If we had the ears to hear, then we would hear a fearful cacophony of anguished voices.

We watch the news on our televisions. We hear stories of oppression. We see pictures of poverty. And we turn away. "Am I my brother's keeper?" Of course we can't meet every need. But we can do something: "Listen!"

Or we hear of Christians being persecuted. The apostle John says Cain killed Abel because Abel was righteous, and then equates Cain with all those who hate the church (1 John 3 v 12-13). Abel is still being murdered by Cain.

∾

Christmas is the story of a better Cain. "Am I my brother's keeper?" says Cain. He won't accept responsibility—even though he's the one who has murdered his brother. Jesus is a very different older brother. He doesn't walk away. He entered our world at Christmas to take responsibility for his brothers and sisters—even though he was the one we would murder.

But Christmas is also the story of a better Abel. "You have come," says the writer of Hebrews, "... to Jesus the mediator of a new covenant, and to the sprinkled blood that speaks a better word than the blood of Abel" (Hebrews 12 v 23-24).

Abel's blood cries out for justice. And rightly so. And Abel represents all the victims of oppression across the centuries. They demand justice. And often we raise our voices with them. We long for justice to be done. We long for evil to be punished and for wrongs to be righted.

The problem is we're not only victims. We are also perpetrators. We may not have killed someone in a field. But we've walked away. "Am I my brother's keeper?" We've failed to take responsibility. Or we've hated people in our hearts. And Jesus says that before God hatred and murder are the same thing (Matthew 5 v 21-22). The only difference between the person who murders and the person with murderous thoughts is a lack of opportunity or a fear of the consequences.

All of which means the blood of Abel cries out *against us!*

But the blood of Jesus is different. Better. The writer of Hebrews has the tabernacle in mind. The high priest came before God on behalf of the people through sprinkled blood. The people deserved to die for their crimes, but an animal died in their place. Its blood represented its forfeited life. This was the basis by which the people could relate to God. And it was this transaction—a life for a life— that the sprinkled blood pictured. But the blood of animals was just a pointer or promise. The reality was Jesus.

The blood of Abel cries out for justice and that justice was exacted at the cross. Jesus died in our place. Our crimes were punished. As a result the blood of Jesus represents the basis on which we can come before God.

The blood of Abel cries out, *Justice!*

Can you hear it? *Can you hear the blood of Abel?*

The blood of Jesus cries out, *Mercy!*

Can you hear it? *Can you hear the blood of Jesus?*

∽

Meditate

You have come … to Jesus the mediator of a new covenant, and to the sprinkled blood that speaks a better word than the blood of Abel.

Mercy speaks by Jesus' blood,
Hear and sing, ye sons of God,
Justice satisfied indeed,
Christ hath full atonement made.

Jesus' blood speaks loud and sweet.
Here all Deity can meet,
And, without a jarring voice,
Welcome Zion to rejoice.

Jesus' blood speaks life and power,
And in every trying hour,
Trusting this almighty voice,
Zion must and shall rejoice.

(William Gadsby, "Mercy speaks by Jesus' blood")

∽

Prayer

Now may the God of peace,
who through the blood of the eternal covenant
brought back from the dead our Lord Jesus,
that great Shepherd of the sheep,
equip you with everything good for doing his will,
and may he work in us what is pleasing to him,
through Jesus Christ,
to whom be glory for ever and ever.
Amen.

(Hebrews 13 v 20-21)

The new ark

*"At that time Jesus came from Nazareth in Galilee
and was baptised by John in the Jordan."*
Mark 1 v 9

Storyline
*Genesis 6 v 5 – 7 v 24; Exodus 1 v 22 – 2 v 10
and Exodus 14*

I used to live on the coast. During storms the waves would hit the
sea wall and shoot several metres up into the sky. Rocks the size
of your fist were left strewn across the road. Those brave enough
or foolish enough to look over the railings saw a dark, churning,
chaotic mass of water. For all its mesmeric beauty, no one was in
any doubt—this was dangerous.

Many years ago in the days of Noah, the whole world was
overtaken by a flood. A dark, churning, chaotic mass of water
covered everything. The worst of it was that this was not some freak
act of nature. It was an act of divine judgment. God's heart was so
troubled at the evil of humanity that he wiped us from the face of
the earth. Not a story we associate with Christmas. But this is part
of the Christmas story just as much as trees and tinsel. More so.

Because floating on top of the watery judgment of God was

Noah's ark. God in his grace was preserving eight people and a menagerie of animals. It was an act of salvation—a new beginning.

Many years later the king of Egypt decreed that every newborn Hebrew boy should be thrown into the River Nile. One Hebrew family kept their boy hidden. But that soon proved impossible. So they placed him in a basket and released him to float down the river. An Egyptian princess found him and had pity on him, and he was saved. The boy was called Moses. In this story, the literal term for his basket is "ark". Just as Noah was saved from water in an ark, so was Moses. It was an act of salvation—a new beginning.

Eighty years later Moses led God's people out of Egyptian slavery—except that, as soon as they left, the king of Egypt changed his mind. The Egyptian army was sent to bring them back. The Israelites found themselves caught between an advancing army and the Red Sea. There was no way out.

But, at God's command, Moses struck the sea with his staff. The waters parted and Moses led his people through to safety. The Egyptian army followed. But as soon as Israel was safe, the sea closed up again. The soldiers were overwhelmed by a dark, churning, chaotic mass of water. Another act of watery judgment from which God's people were kept safe. It was another act of salvation—a new beginning.

∽

2,000 years later, another baby was born. Another deliverer: Jesus.

Mark skips the nativity story. There's no room in his Gospel for inns with no room. He doesn't tell the story of shepherds and Magi to explain the coming of the Christ-child. Instead he skips forward to John the Baptist and the baptism of Jesus. He explains the coming of Jesus by echoing these stories of watery judgment.

Jesus enters the water of the River Jordan. John's baptism, explains Mark, was *"a baptism of repentance for the forgiveness of sins"* (Mark 1 v 4). It was full of symbols of new beginnings. The prophet Isaiah had spoken of a new exodus through water to a new beginning (Isaiah 43 v 16-21). People were enacting their need for this new beginning by being baptised. In the first century, baptism was how Gentiles converted to Judaism. So for Jews to be baptised was a humble recognition that they, too, needed to become a new people.

When Jesus entered the waters of the Jordan, he was associating with sinners. He was without sin. But he identified with us. He enfolded himself in the waters of God's judgment. It was a powerful symbol of what was to come. In Mark 10 v 38 Jesus described his death as a baptism. At the cross he enfolded himself in God's judgment. He took the judgment we deserve; he stood in our place. And then three days later he rose as the promise of new life for all who have faith in him. Just as Moses had led the people through God's judgment to safety, so Jesus will lead us through judgment to safety. It is the ultimate act of salvation—the ultimate new beginning.

This is what we enact in baptism. We symbolically follow the journey of Jesus through the judgment of death and out again to new life. His journey becomes our journey. Just as he associated with sinners in *his* baptism, so we associate with *him* in our baptism. 1 Peter 3 v 20-21 says:

> *In the days of Noah ... in [the ark] only a few people, eight in all, were saved through water, and this water symbolises baptism that now saves you also—not the removal of dirt from the body*

but the pledge of a clear conscience towards God. It saves you by the resurrection of Jesus Christ.

Jesus is the true ark. We're kept safe in him. We pass through judgment in him and come to rest in a world made new.

Jesus is the true Moses. Paul says the Israelites "were all baptised into Moses in the cloud and in the sea" (1 Corinthians 10 v 2). Moses led them through judgment to freedom. In the same way, Jesus leads us through judgment to safety.

The stories of Noah and Moses converge in the birth of Jesus—and your story converges with all of those stories too if you've been baptised.

So when you get a Christmas card depicting the baby in the manger think of Moses in his "ark", kept safe from watery judgment. And remember that Jesus keeps us safe from judgment. Remember what Mark thinks is important about the coming of Jesus: Jesus will plunge into the chaos of God's judgment to lead you to safety.

And when you feel overwhelmed by your sin, or when Satan points out your failures, think of your baptism. Jesus gave us baptism as a promise that he has kept us safe through judgment and he will lead us to freedom.

∽

Meditate

At that time Jesus came from Nazareth in Galilee
and was baptised by John in the Jordan.

Many waters cannot quench love;
rivers cannot sweep it away.

(Song of Songs 8 v 7)

∽

Prayer

Father God,
just as Noah was kept safe
from the waters of judgment in the ark;
just as Moses was kept safe
from the waters of judgment in the basket;
just as Israel was kept safe
from the waters of judgment in Moses;
so may we be kept safe
from the reality of judgment in Christ.
When we fall into sin,
may our baptism be to us
the pledge of a clear conscience,
and the promise of salvation
by the resurrection of Jesus.
Amen.

The hope of 6 the nations

*"Magi from the east came to Jerusalem and
asked, 'Where is the one who has been born king of the
Jews? We saw his star when it rose and have come to
worship him.'"*
Matthew 2 v 2

Storyline
Genesis 11 v 1-9; Matthew 2 v 1-12 and Luke 2 v 22-35

Santa Claus is a Dutch version of St. Nicholas, who was a Turkish bishop. Decorated trees come from Germany, supposedly introduced to Britain by Prince Albert, Queen Victoria's husband. The date of December 25th was probably chosen to replace Roman mid-winter festivities.

The tradition of wrapping a red ribbon round an orange and sticking a candle in the top to create a "Christingle" was invented in 1747 by John de Watteville, a Moravian pastor. The British can take the credit (or blame) for Christmas cards, created to promote the postal service.

Our contemporary Christmas is a truly international affair.

> *Now the whole world had one language and a common speech.*
> *As people moved eastward, they found a plain in Shinar and*
> *settled there.* Genesis 11 v 1

So begins Genesis 11. Adam and Eve were sent east out of Eden. Their son Cain was exiled east of Eden. And here humanity was still moving eastward, away from God.

God commanded humanity to fill the earth. Had they done so, then a diversity of cultures and languages would have developed. But instead, humanity comes together on the plain of Shinar. They refuse to scatter (v 4). So instead of diversity, there is just *"one language and a common speech"*. It's the first declaration of empire, and empires ever since have tried to impose uniformity on their subjects.

> *Then they said, "Come, let us build ourselves a city, with a*
> *tower that reaches to the heavens, so that we may make a name*
> *for ourselves."*   v 4

Humanity was made in the image of God to reflect God's glory in the world. But instead, the whole world comes together in defiance of God for its own glory.

Meanwhile, the LORD "came down to see the city and the tower the people were building" (v 5). Humanity says, "Come, let us … [reach] to the heavens". In response the triune God says, "Come, let us go down" (v 7). God comes down to judge humanity. He confuses their language, forcing them to scatter. The place is called "Babel", which sounds like "confused" in Hebrew. Think of the word "babble" and you get the idea. As a result, God accelerates the command to fill the earth and develop diverse cultures.

∽

Today we live with this wonderful diversity of cultures. Just think of the food you enjoy. Italian pasta. Indian curry. French casseroles. Mexican fajitas. British cakes. *What's not to love?!* But along with this diversity we get division: racism, discrimination, war.

At the first Christmas, the triune God again says, *Come, let us go down.* But instead of God coming down to judge humanity, he comes down in the person of Jesus to save humanity. And to unite us in a new humanity.

That's the meaning of the Magi. Matthew's Gospel tells their story:

> *After Jesus was born in Bethlehem in Judea, during the time of King Herod, Magi from the east came to Jerusalem.*
>
> Matthew 2 v 1

Where do they come from? *From the east!* At Babel, humanity was moving eastward, away from God. Now humanity (represented by the Magi) are coming from the east, back to God. Matthew has just told us that the baby Jesus is "Immanuel"—God with us (1 v 23). The Magi come, not to make a name for themselves, but to bow down and worship God-in-Christ (v 11).

Jew and Gentile were divided by bitter centuries of hostility. But here in Bethlehem Mary, Joseph and the Magi stand together around God-in-the-manger. Here in miniature is a picture of the empire of Jesus. The peoples of the world are united in the worship of Christ.

So Matthew's Gospel begins with the nations coming to worship Jesus. And it ends with Jesus telling his disciples to "go and make disciples of all nations" (28 v 19). Instead of *coming together,* Christians are *sent out* into the world. We are scattered throughout the earth to gather in the nations.

Jesus reverses the curse of Babel. Instead of the nations being scattered, they are brought together around his manger and around his throne. And that process is taking place through the mission of the church.

~

Simeon expresses the same message in Luke's Gospel. Simeon was a "righteous and devout" man (Luke 2 v 25). He was waiting for "the consolation of Israel" and the Holy Spirit had revealed to him that he would not die "before he had seen the Lord's Messiah" (v 25-26).

When Mary and Joseph brought Jesus to be consecrated in the Jerusalem Temple, Simeon took him in his arms. He was, Luke tells us, "moved by the Spirit" (v 27). He realised that this was the child who would fulfil the promise of God. As he held the infant Jesus close, Simeon described him as "a light for revelation to the Gentiles, and the glory of your people Israel" (v 32). Simeon was echoing Isaiah 49 v 6. The word "Gentiles" is the word "nations". Jesus is the light not only of Israel, but of the world.

~

The empire of Jesus does not impose uniformity. This is not an empire of "one language and a common speech". Instead there are people from every tribe, language, people and nation. It's an empire that celebrates diversity. The Magi bring with them "treasures"— "gifts of gold, frankincense and myrrh". The diversity of the nations is presented to God-in-the-manger just as one day "the glory and honour of the nations will be brought into" the city of the Lamb (Revelation 21 v 26).

Christmas is a great opportunity to invite people from other cultures to share your family Christmas, especially those, like refugees or international students, who feel far from home. Or perhaps this Christmas you could explore a Christmas tradition from another culture. But whatever you do and whoever you are, remember and marvel that brothers and sisters from every corner of the planet will be celebrating with joy the light of the world.

∽

Meditate

Magi from the east came to Jerusalem and asked, "Where is the one who has been born king of the Jews? We saw his star when it rose and have come to worship him."

I cannot tell why he, whom angels worship,
Should set his love upon the sons of men.
Or why, as Shepherd, he should seek the wand'rers
To bring them back, they know not how or when.
But this I know, that he was born of Mary,
When Bethl'hem's manger was his only home,
And that he lived at Nazareth and laboured,
And so the Saviour, Saviour of the world, is come.

I cannot tell how he will win the nations,
How he will claim his earthly heritage,
How satisfy the needs and aspirations
Of east and west, of sinner and of sage.
But this I know, all flesh shall see his glory,
And he shall reap the harvest he has sown,
And some glad day his sun shall shine in splendour
When he the Saviour, Saviour of the world, is known.

(From "I cannot tell" by William Fullerton)

Prayer

Thou, whose almighty word
Chaos and darkness heard,
And took their flight;
Hear us, we humbly pray,
And, where the gospel day
Sheds not its glorious ray,
Let there be light!
Amen.

(From "Thou, whose almighty word" by John Marriott)

The ultimate punchline

*"Sarah said, 'God has brought me laughter, and
everyone who hears about this will laugh with me.'"*
Genesis 21 v 6

Storyline
Genesis 18 v 1-15; 1 Samuel 1 – 2 and Luke 1 v 5-56

So what I meant to say was, "Lawfully wedded wife". But what
came out was, "Awfully wedded wife". The wedding descended
into chaos.

Have you ever said something in deadly earnest, only to find it
sets everyone off laughing? For a moment you wonder why. And
then you realise your words came out wrong and what you said was
preposterous.

It happened to God. Twice. But God didn't get his words wrong.
He was being deadly earnest. It was Abraham and Sarah who thought
it sounded preposterous.

God tells Abraham that his wife will have a son. In fact she's
going to become "the mother of nations". "Abraham," we read,
"fell face down; he laughed" (Genesis 17 v 17). Abraham fell about
laughing, we might say—or we might text ROFL (rolling on the
floor laughing). To Abraham the thought of Sarah having a son

sounded preposterous. Abraham was too old. Sarah was too old. And Sarah had been barren all her life. Abraham said to himself, "Will a son be born to a man a hundred years old? Will Sarah bear a child at the age of ninety?" (v 17)

Not long afterwards three strangers visit Abraham. Abraham offers them hospitality as was customary. At the beginning of the story they appear as "three men". But the writer tips us off that this is an appearance of the LORD, and by the end of the story it is the LORD who speaks. And this is what he says: "I will surely return to you about this time next year, and Sarah your wife will have a son" (Genesis 18 v 10).

It turns out Sarah has been eavesdropping and overhears this conversation. Just in case we'd forgotten, the writer reminds us that Abraham and Sarah are too old to have children. "So Sarah laughed to herself as she thought, 'After I am worn out and my lord is old, will I now have this pleasure?'" (v 12) It's a preposterous idea. It sounds like a joke. The obvious response is laughter.

Sarah's laughter does not go unnoticed.

> *Then the LORD said to Abraham, "Why did Sarah laugh and say, 'Will I really have a child, now that I am old?' Is anything too hard for the LORD?"*　　　　　　　　　　v 13-14

This is a joke on a global scale. At stake is not just Sarah's pleasure. At stake is the future of humanity. For God had promised that all nations would be blessed through Abraham's offspring. God promised a Saviour would come from the family of Abraham. But Abraham has no family—not of his own. It looks like the LORD has made a terrible mistake. He has staked the future of humanity on a barren, past-it couple.

What a joke.

∾

But God gets the last laugh—quite literally. For a year later Sarah does indeed give birth to a son. And the name of the child is "Isaac", which means "laughter".

> *Now the LORD was gracious to Sarah as he had said, and the LORD did for Sarah what he had promised. Sarah became pregnant and bore a son to Abraham in his old age, at the very time God had promised him.*   Genesis 21 v 1-2

"As he had said … what he had promised … at the very time God had promised." Let no one doubt this is God's doing. And that's the point. God was signalling at the start of the story of salvation that the future of humanity does not depend on human power or goodness. It depends on his power and his grace.

Indeed, just in case we don't get the message, God repeats the feat in the next generation. Isaac's wife, Rebekah, is also barren until God gives her a child. Then he does it again the generation after that. Jacob's second wife, Rachel, is barren until God gives her a child. It is a pattern that is repeated throughout Scripture. At crucial moments throughout the Bible story, a key child is born of a previously barren woman. The judge Samson is born to a barren couple. The prophet Samuel is born to a barren wife: Hannah. John the Baptist is born to Zechariah and Elizabeth, an elderly barren couple. What does this mean? Why has God repeatedly done this?

And then it all becomes clear. God goes one better as the Messiah—the ultimate saviour—is born to a virgin.

∾

When barren Hannah finally gives birth, she sings a song (1 Samuel 2 v 1-10). And Mary's song (the "Magnificat" of Luke 1 v 46-55) is full of echoes of Hannah's song. The songs link their experiences. The birth of Jesus to a virgin is the ultimate display of God's creative and re-creative power.

This is the significance of the virgin birth. It's the ultimate sign that salvation is all God's work and not the result of human potency. Perhaps that's why some people deny the virgin birth. They want to retain the idea that human beings have a role in determining their future. They laugh at the virgin birth, just as Abraham and Sarah did when promised a child.

Abraham is asked by his visitor, "Is anything too hard for the Lord?" (18 v 14) When the angel tells Mary the Holy Spirit will come on her in power, he adds, "For nothing will be impossible with God" (Luke 1 v 37, ESV). Is anything too hard for God? No, nothing is too hard for God.

God gets the last laugh time and again. But the lovely thing about this joke is that we can join in the laughter. God gets the last laugh, but he shares that laughter with us. "Sarah said, 'God has brought me laughter, and everyone who hears about this will laugh with me'" (Genesis 21 v 6). The "joke" is that humanity appeared to have no future, but God has given us a future. The joy of Isaac's birth is the joy of humanity's rebirth. And this joy is infectious. When you truly hear this good news you respond with joy.

What will the source of your joy and laughter be in the next few weeks? Video clips on your Facebook feed? Old comedy shows? Children opening presents? Or will you radiate joy because you know how unbelievably good the good news is…

∽

Meditate

Sarah said, "God has brought me laughter, and everyone who hears about this will laugh with me."

My soul doth magnify the Lord:
and my spirit hath rejoiced in God my Saviour.
For he hath regarded:
the lowliness of his hand-maiden.
For behold, from henceforth:
all generations shall call me blessed.
For he that is mighty hath magnified me:
and holy is his Name.
And his mercy is on them that fear him:
throughout all generations.
He hath shewed strength with his arm:
he hath scattered the proud in the imagination of their hearts.
He hath put down the mighty from their seat:
and hath exalted the humble and meek.
He hath filled the hungry with good things:
and the rich he hath sent empty away.
He remembering his mercy hath helped his servant Israel:
as he promised to our forefathers, Abraham and his seed, for ever.

(The "Magnificat" or Song of Mary from The Book of Common Prayer)

∽

Prayer

Father, we pray that out of your glorious riches
you may strengthen us with power
through your Spirit in our inner being,
so that Christ may dwell in our hearts through faith.
And we pray that we, being rooted and established in love,
may have power, together with all your holy people,
to grasp how wide and long and high and deep is the love of Christ,
and to know this love that surpasses knowledge—that we may be filled to
the measure of all your fulness.

Now to him who is able to do immeasurably more
than all we ask or imagine,
according to his power that is at work within us,
to him be glory in the church and in Christ Jesus
throughout all generations, for ever and ever! Amen.

(Adapted from Ephesians 3 v 14-21)

The justice of God

"Will not the Judge of all the earth do right?"
Genesis 18 v 25

Storyline
Genesis 18 v 16-33

I talk to myself all the time. There's an internal dialogue going on inside my head when I'm around other people. But as soon as I'm on my own, it becomes an external conversation. I confess that I talk out loud to myself. I have to be careful turning street corners in case someone coming the other way overhears me and decides I'm crazy. Maybe I am.

In Genesis 18 God talks to himself. Except of course that with God it's not a monologue, but a trilogue between the three Persons of the Trinity. The LORD in human form is visiting Abraham and has just promised Abraham that he will have a son in a year's time. Then God says to himself (or themselves), "Shall I hide from Abraham what I am about to do?" (v 17) He continues:

Abraham will surely become a great and powerful nation, and all nations on earth will be blessed through him. For I have chosen him, so that he will direct his children and his household after him to keep the way of the LORD by doing what is right and just, so that the LORD will bring about for Abraham what he has promised him. Genesis 18 v 18-19

Because of the promise Abraham has just received, he will become a great nation. But not only that, *all* nations will be blessed through Abraham. The primary way that will happen is that God's promised Saviour will come from the family of Abraham. The offspring of Abraham will save the world. But God highlights *another* way that Abraham will bless the nations. Abraham's family will reflect the character of the LORD. They will model the righteousness and justice of God.

Back in the Garden of Eden, Satan had insinuated that God's rule was tyrannical and corrupt. Satan persuaded humanity that we would be better off without God in charge. In reality, far from being freer, we have became enslaved to sin. Sin crouches at our door, ready to rule us. But the lie of Satan lingers. Indeed, it has become the central myth by which we live our lives. We're persuaded, and so we live in rebellion against God. God is a tyrant, we suppose, and we're better off without him.

Abraham's job was to dispel this lie. His ways were to reflect God's ways. And so he would bless the nations. He would show the true nature of God's rule. He would model the justice of God.

～

But is God just? God's justice is immediately thrown into question by his next pronouncement. God is on a mission to examine Sodom and Gomorrah. And their very existence is on the line.

So Abraham tests the justice of God. If he is to model it, then he must be confident in it. In an audacious conversation, he questions God's justice. *"Will you sweep away the righteous with the wicked?"*

he asks. *"What if there are fifty righteous people in the city?"* (v 23-24) The LORD promises to spare the city if there are fifty righteous people within it. Abraham goes further. What about forty-five? God will spare the city for the sake of forty-five righteous people. The dialogue continues. What about forty? What about thirty? What about twenty? What about ten? God says, "For the sake of ten, I will not destroy it" (v 32).

And then the conversation stops. "What about five? What about one?" we want to ask. But nothing. All we read is, "When the LORD had finished speaking with Abraham, he left, and Abraham returned home" (v 33).

What happens next is that two angels accompanying the LORD go into the city of Sodom. Only Lot (Abraham's nephew) and his family are found to be right with God—and then only because they trust in God. Even their trust has to be urged on them as the angels usher them out of the doomed city. And even then Lot's wife can't believe it, and is caught up in the destruction as she becomes a pillar of salt when she turns back. Nobody righteous is left in the city and God's judgment falls.

And so the question remains: will God spare the city for the sake of one righteous person?

2,000 years later, the answer to that question lies in the manger.

∽

Jesus comes as the offspring of Abraham. He is the Saviour promised from the family of Abraham. He is the one through whom all the nations will be blessed. When John the Baptist is born, Zechariah sings:

Praise be to the Lord, the God of Israel,
because he has come to his people and redeemed them.
He has raised up a horn of salvation for us …
to remember his holy covenant,
the oath he swore to our father Abraham:
to rescue us from the hand of our enemies,
and to enable us to serve him without fear
in holiness and righteousness before him all our days.

Luke 1 v 68-69, 72-75

Jesus is the One who perfectly embodies the character of God. In Jesus we see the goodness of God's reign. He models the righteousness of God and enables God's people to serve God in holiness and righteousness.

And then Jesus dies on the cross, "the righteous for the unrighteous, to bring you to God" (1 Peter 3 v 18). The just for the unjust. And the question—will God spare the wicked for the sake of one righteous person?—gets its ultimate answer. Yes. It is answered in a way that goes far beyond anything we might have predicted.

Just as one trespass resulted in condemnation for all people, so
also one righteous act resulted in justification and life for all
people. For just as through the disobedience of the one man the
many were made sinners, so also through the obedience of the one
man the many will be made righteous. Romans 5 v 18-19

Where does that leave us? We are made righteous (right with God) through faith alone in Christ alone. But as a result, we're enabled to model the righteousness of God and so bless the nations by dispelling Satan's lie.

The festive season can be a time when we just want to relax—

put our feet up, enjoy some comfort, and look after ourselves for a change. But this Christmas, if you are a parent, will you direct your children and your household to keep the way of the LORD by doing what is right and just? And all of us, will we bless those around us by reflecting the character of God and modelling the goodness of his reign?

∽

Meditate

Will not the Judge of all the earth do right?

What can I give him, poor as I am?
If I were a shepherd, I would bring a lamb.
If I were a wise man, I would do my part.
Yet what I can I give him: give my heart.

(From "In the bleak midwinter" by Christina Rossetti)

∽

Prayer

Inspire and strengthen us by your Holy Spirit, O Lord God,
to seek your will and uphold your honour in all things:
in the purity and joy of our homes,
in the trust and fellowship of our common life,
in daily service of the good,
after the pattern and in the power of your Son,
our Lord and Saviour, Jesus Christ.
Amen.

(Jeremy Taylor)

The refugee

"A voice is heard in Ramah, mourning and great weeping, Rachel weeping for her children and refusing to be comforted, because they are no more."
Jeremiah 31 v 15

Storyline
Exodus 1 v 1-22 and Matthew 2 v 13-18

We associate Christmas with family. Often children are the focus of our celebrations. "It's for the children," we say as we hand over our credit card or don our flashing reindeer antlers.

But the first Christmas was a terrifying time for the children of Bethlehem. King Herod had heard that a king had been born, a rival to his dynasty. So he ordered the massacre of every infant boy. Imagine how that unfolded. Soldiers streamed into the town unannounced and started raiding every home. Doors were kicked open, rooms were searched, and babies dragged from their mothers so soldiers could slash them with swords. Imagine the cries of anguish repeated in home after home.

And this was not the first time it had happened.

◡

Abraham's child became a family. His grandson Jacob was renamed "Israel". Jacob was, quite literally, the father of the nation. The nation bears his name, Israel. But then it looked as if Jacob's family might be wiped out by famine: the end of a family, but also the end of God's promises.

As the story unfolds in Genesis, God orchestrates events so that one of Jacob's sons, Joseph, becomes the key figure in Egypt. As a result the family is able to find refuge there. Time passed and the family became a great nation. So great that the Egyptians feared this nation within a nation. So the king of Egypt ordered the massacre of every newborn male Hebrew infant. It was an attempt to bring the nation to an end and with it the promises of God. But the opening chapter of Exodus recounts how the Hebrew midwives had the courage to subvert Pharaoh's plan. Moses escaped in his "ark" and within a generation he was leading God's people to freedom.

∽

When Herod ordered the massacre of the Bethlehem babies, he was repeating what Pharaoh had attempted centuries before. As Matthew describes Herod's massacre, he quotes from Jeremiah 31 v 15:

> *A voice is heard in Ramah, mourning and great weeping,*
> *Rachel weeping for her children and refusing to be comforted,*
> *because they are no more.*

Rachel was Jacob's wife. If Jacob was the father of the nation, then Rachel was the mother of the nation. And perhaps she represents all the mothers of Israel, weeping for their lost children. In the ninth century BC and then again in the sixth century BC, the people of God were defeated and dragged off into exile, the northern tribes to Assyria and the southern tribes to Babylon. Ramah is near to where Rachel was buried. It's also a few miles north of Jerusalem on the road towards Babylon. It's as if Rachel weeps from her grave as she sees her "children" heading off into exile. The nation has no future. It's being dismantled and disbanded.

But Jeremiah's description of Rachel's tears comes in a passage full of promise. God responds:

> *"Restrain your voice from weeping and your eyes from tears,*
> *for your work will be rewarded," declares the LORD.*
> *"They will return from the land of the enemy.*
> *So there is hope for your descendants," declares the LORD.*
> *"Your children will return to their own land."*

Jeremiah 31 v 16-17

The planned massacre by Pharaoh, the exile to Assyria and Babylon, and the massacre by Herod (plus the proposed massacre of Jews which was thwarted by Esther) are all part of the same pattern—the same thread of the story. Behind them stands Satan, intent on destroying God's people so he can destroy God's plan. If Satan could obliterate the people from whom the Saviour would come, then perhaps he could stop the serpent-crusher, who would be born to destroy him. But time and again God thwarts Satan's designs.

Finally, at the first Christmas, the Saviour arrives and again Satan, through Herod, attempts to obliterate the Saviour. But God warns Joseph in a dream and Jesus escapes to Egypt with his family. Once again God preserves his people and protects his plan of salvation. As Matthew 2 v 14-15 points out, Jesus was a refugee in Egypt just as Israel had been hundreds of years before.

∾

"Restrain your voice from weeping and your eyes from tears." There is a time to weep. When we see the brokenness of our world, when we see the suffering of children, when we see Satan's continued opposition to the plan of salvation, when God's people are being persecuted—we rightly cry out to God.

There is a time to weep. But Christmas is not that time—not when we see the promise of Christmas. Satan doesn't get the last word. God's promises are sure. God has preserved the descendants of Abraham. Jesus has come. And Jesus has defeated Satan. He has crushed the serpent's head. Satan may still rage against the church, but his days are numbered—he has been mortally wounded. There may be times when the church feels vulnerable, but the gates of hell will not prevail against it.

∽

Remember, too, the refugees of our generation. Remember the children today fleeing massacres. There may be Christmas activities planned for refugees in your area which you could support as a family. Remember that Jesus was once one of those children.

Meditate
A voice is heard in Ramah, mourning and great weeping,
Rachel weeping for her children and refusing to be comforted,
because they are no more.

It came upon the midnight clear,
That glorious song of old,
From angels bending near the earth
To touch their harps of gold:
"Peace on the earth, good will to men

From heaven's all-gracious King."
The world in solemn stillness lay
To hear the angels sing.

And ye, beneath life's crushing load,
Whose forms are bending low,
Who toil along the climbing way
With painful steps and slow,
Look now, for glad and golden hours
Come swiftly on the wing.
Oh rest beside the weary road
And hear the angels sing!

(From "It came upon the midnight clear" by Edmund Sears)

~

Prayer

Father God,
just as your Son was once a refugee,
fleeing the violence of a tyrant,
so we pray for refugees today.
May they be protected when they journey,
may they be welcomed when they arrive,
and may they discover the hope found in Jesus
so their weeping turns to joy.
Amen.

The rock

"They all ate the same spiritual food and drank the same spiritual drink; for they drank from the spiritual rock that accompanied them, and that rock was Christ."
1 Corinthians 10 v 3-4

Storyline
Exodus 17 v 1-7

"It's not the right type." "Do we have to have your parents over again?" "Will you please just give me five minutes' peace." "Why can't Jonny clear the table?" "I can't believe you're making me play charades." Christmas and grumbling go together almost as surely as Christmas and turkey.

Grumbling, of course, is what other people do. What *I* do is make legitimate observations and justified criticism. And I'm sure that you, dear reader, are the same.

Or are we just fooling ourselves? Let's put it to the test. Challenge yourself to make only positive comments this Christmas. Let's call it the "Ephesians 4" challenge: Ephesians 4 v 29 says, "Do not let any unwholesome talk come out of your mouths, but only what is helpful for building others up according to their needs, that it may benefit those who listen." Alongside this we read, "Get rid of all bitterness, rage and anger, brawling and slander, along with every form of malice" (v 31). Keep asking yourself, "Will what I'm about to say build people up? Will it benefit them?"

In case we're tempted to think of this as a light-hearted matter, in the middle of these exhortations Paul says, "And do not grieve the Holy Spirit of God, with whom you were sealed for the day of redemption" (v 30). Unhelpful talk and a bitter attitude grieves God the Holy Spirit.

⁀

Israel had a grumbling problem. God dramatically rescued them from slavery in Egypt. He led them through the Red Sea to freedom. On the eastern shore they sang his praises. *"In your unfailing love you will lead the people you have redeemed,"* they sang (Exodus 15 v 13).

But just three days later they were grumbling against Moses when they couldn't find water (Exodus 15 v 24). Three days. That was all it took to go from praise to grumbling.

To be honest, that's good going compared to me. On Sunday morning I can be singing God's praises. By Sunday afternoon I'm in a foul mood, and filled with complaints. I might not always cite God on my charge sheet. But I'm not content with the way he's organised my life.

What did God do in response to the grumbling of the Israelites? Zap them with a thunderbolt? Abandon them in the desert? No—he graciously provided them with water.

And yet, a few days later the Israelites were at it again. This time they grumbled because they had no food (Exodus 16). Obviously having no food is a problem! No one likes being hungry. But by now God had an impressive track record of providing for his people. But the people didn't trust God and so they grumbled.

What did God do in response? He graciously provided them with manna from heaven.

What happened next? The Israelites grumbled for a third time (Exodus 17 v 1-7). They grumbled because they had no water. Again! They didn't trust God even though manna was still appearing from heaven every morning! Every morning they woke up to this reminder of God's faithfulness.

$$\sim\!\!\mathcal{O}$$

In the first two stories we're told that God tested the Israelites (15 v 25; 16 v 4). But the third time round they tested God (17 v 2). They put God on trial. What did God do in response? He convened the courtroom.

> *The LORD answered Moses, "Go out in front of the people. Take with you some of the elders of Israel and take in your hand the staff with which you struck the Nile, and go. I will stand there before you by the rock at Horeb."*   Exodus 17 v 5-6

Try to picture the scene. On the one side are the elders, representing the Israelites. On the other side is God. Obviously you can't see God, but he's represented by the rock. In the middle is Moses. For the purposes of the exercise, he's the judge. Indeed, he holds in his hand his staff—the staff through which the plague-judgments on Egypt were brought. So the staff represents the judgment of the court. All this is played out in front of the people. They're there to witness what happens.

What's the verdict going to be? God has faithfully rescued his people from Egypt, led them through the desert, and provided water and bread along the way. The people have moaned and complained—not once, not twice, but three times. They've failed to trust God. It's obvious who's guilty. The outcome of the trial is clear. God will be vindicated and his people will be judged.

And then God says to Moses, "Strike the rock" (17 v 6). The staff of judgment falls, but it falls on God instead of on his people.

It's an extraordinary moment. I like to imagine a pause with the staff suspended above Moses' head. And the people cower in fear as they expect the staff to fall on their representatives. Then Moses' arms start to fall and he crashes the staff down on the opposite side—against the rock, against God. Everyone feels shock and horror and relief—all rolled into one.

Then water gushes from the rock for the people to drink. God takes the judgment his people deserve and in return they experience his blessing. *Wow!*

∾

"That rock was Christ," says Paul in 1 Corinthians 10 v 4. What happened in the desert was a symbol. The whole thing was choreographed as a piece of vivid visual theatre—for them then, and for us now. The reality took place at the cross. As Jesus hung on the cross, the staff of God's judgment came crashing down on Jesus. It was as if God stood as judge, and before him on one side was humanity—guilty and deserving of judgment. On the other side was Jesus—innocent and deserving to be vindicated. For a moment the staff of God's judgment was suspended as the sky turned black. And then his judgment fell on his Son in our place.

The baby in the manger came to be the true Rock. He came to bear the judgment we deserve. As a result, blessing gushes from Christ to God's people.

∾

There will be moments this Christmas when you want to grumble. I can guarantee that not everything will go your way! In those moments remember Jesus the Rock. Think of the blessing that gushes in your direction because he hung on the cross. The circumstances won't magically transform. But whatever is annoying you might suddenly not seem quite so important.

∽

Meditate

They all ate the same spiritual food and drank the same spiritual drink;
for they drank from the spiritual rock that accompanied them,
and that rock was Christ.

Rock of Ages, cleft for me,
Let me hide myself in thee.
Let the water and the blood,
From thy riven side which flowed,
Be of sin the double cure,
Cleanse me from its guilt and power.

(From "Rock of ages" by Augustus Montague Toplady)

∽

Prayer

Thou that hast giv'n so much to me,
Give one thing more, a grateful heart …
Not thankful when it pleaseth me;
As if thy blessings had spare days:
But such a heart, whose pulse may be
thy praise.

Amen.

(George Herbert)

The tabernacle

*"The Word became flesh
and made his dwelling among us.
We have seen his glory."*
John 1 v 14

Storyline
Exodus 40

Do you have a favourite moment in a movie? Maybe the moment Gandalf and the riders of Rohan appear on the ridge to save Helm's Deep in *The Two Towers*. Or maybe the end of *An Officer and a Gentlemen* when Zack, in full military uniform, carries Paula out of the factory. Or the moment Luke Skywalker destroys the Death Star in the original *Star Wars* movie.

There's no shortage of dramatic moments in the book of Exodus. The burning bush. The head-to-head confrontation between Moses and Pharaoh. The staff of Moses spreading blood throughout the Nile. Plagues of frogs, gnats, flies, disease on livestock, boils, hail, locusts, darkness and death. The pillars of fire and cloud. The parting of the Red Sea. The fireworks and thunderstorm at Mount Sinai. Even with all this by way of prelude, the end is no anti-climax. In great detail God has described the tabernacle which the Israelites are to build (Exodus 25-31), and in matching detail the construction of the tabernacle has been described (Exodus 35-40). Then finally we read:

> *The cloud covered the tent of meeting, and the glory of the*
> *LORD filled the tabernacle. Moses could not enter the tent of*
> *meeting because the cloud had settled on it, and the glory of the*
> *LORD filled the tabernacle.*   Exodus 40 v 34-35

What a sight that must have been—the whole tabernacle glowing with radiant light. Or was it fizzing?

For a generation the Israelites saw a pillar of cloud over the tabernacle by day and a pillar of fire by night. Sometimes the cloud would lift and lead them. At other times it settled over the tabernacle. The Israelites set up camp with three tribes on each side of the tabernacle, so the tabernacle was always in the centre.

The tabernacle was a giant symbol covered in more symbols. The character and purposes of God were encoded in its design and furnishings.

It spoke of God's inaccessibility. The innermost part of the tabernacle, the Most Holy Place, was separated by a thick curtain. Woven into the design of the curtain were cherubim, evoking the memory of the angelic guardians that prevented Adam and Eve returning to the Garden of Eden.

In front of the curtain was an altar of incense. It was, in effect, a cloud-making machine. The aim was to replicate the experience of Mount Sinai, when God came down in a cloud with thunder and lightning. At Sinai the people were told not even to step onto the mountain, otherwise God would strike out against them. That sense of separation was replicated in the design of the tabernacle. It all added up to a powerful sign that God is so holy that sinful people cannot be in his presence. Approaching him would be like putting tissue paper into a fire.

And yet at the same time, the tabernacle was set up to welcome us into God's presence. A light was always on inside and a table was permanently laid with bread. They weren't for God's benefit—God needs neither light nor food. They were a sign that God's people are invited to eat with him, to share community with him. God's "home" was in the middle of the people's homes. He lived in a tent alongside people living in tents.

Resolving this push-pull tension of God's holy perfection and presence were the sacrifices. It's our sin combined with God's commitment to justice that prevents us coming into God's presence. A sacrifice represented judgment against sin. The animal bore the penalty of death which sinners deserve. As a result the people of Israel were cleansed. But it was all very provisional and merely symbolic. Only the high priest could come into the Most Holy Place and only once a year.

～

In a movie, the moments of greatest drama are sometimes those full of noise and action—two characters argue at full volume perhaps, or bombs go off as the hero escapes through the carnage of falling buildings. But the moments of greatest drama can also be quieter affairs—when all is still and the leading characters speak softly but resolutely of their love or their determination. The stillness and quiet only add to the drama.

The descent of the glory of God on the tabernacle was an example of the former—an explosion of special effects. Matthew 1 v 23 is an example of the latter. Isaiah is quoted: "The virgin will conceive and give birth to a son, and they will call him Immanuel" (which means "God with us")." No one saw or heard the cells combine at the conception of Jesus. Even Mary would have been unaware of the exact moment when it occurred. Or move on nine months. Joseph remembers the dream in which he was told these words and sees the baby asleep in the manger: Immanuel. God is with us and he is lying in the straw.

But, though the moment of conception passed unnoticed and the baby seemed so fragile, there is no drama to match this moment. Nothing speaks more powerfully of the determination of God's love.

ↄ

John 1 v 14 says:

> *The Word became flesh and made his dwelling among us.*
> *We have seen his glory.*

The phrase "made his dwelling" is literally "tabernacled". God pitched his tent among us in the person of his Son. All that the tabernacle symbolised is realised in Jesus. Here in human form is God's intent to live among his people and welcome us into his presence.

And one day, as Jesus died—the ultimate sacrifice—the curtain dividing us from the Most Holy Place was torn in two from top to bottom. The writer of Hebrews says that in Jesus we pass through the curtain into God's presence (Hebrews 10 v 19-22). We do that now every time we pray, and we will do that one day when we stand before God.

ↄ

Meditate

The Word became flesh and made his dwelling among us.
We have seen his glory.

Love came down at Christmas,
Love all lovely, Love divine;
Love was born at Christmas,
Star and angels gave the sign.

Worship we the Godhead,
Love incarnate, Love divine;
Worship we our Jesus:
But wherewith for sacred sign?

Love shall be our token,
Love be yours and love be mine,
Love to God and all men,
Love for plea and gift and sign.

(Christina Rossetti)

Tim Chester

Prayer

Love Divine, all loves excelling,
Joy of heaven, to earth come down,
Fix in us thy humble dwelling,
All thy faithful mercies crown.
Jesus, thou art all compassion,
Pure unbounded love thou art:
Visit us with thy salvation,
Enter every trembling heart.
Amen.

(From "Love divine" by Charles Wesley)

The true people of God

12

"Jesus, full of the Holy Spirit, left the Jordan and was led by the Spirit into the wilderness, where for forty days he was tempted by the devil."

Luke 4 v 1-2

Storyline

Numbers 13 – 14; Luke 3 v 21 – 4 v 13

Who are the true people of God? A long time ago they were the family of Abraham. Later they were the people Moses led out of Egypt—mostly ethnic Hebrews, but with a rag-bag of other people who had joined them.

The prophet Elijah thought he was the only faithful person left, but in fact God had 7,000 people who'd refused to worship Baal (1 Kings 19 v 14, 18). Today the people of God is made up of all who are true followers of Jesus, whether Jew or Gentile.

But there's a very real sense in which the true people of God has only ever been *one person*: Jesus.

Jesus is Immanuel, God-with-us. He's fully God. "God from God, Light from Light, true God from true God; begotten, not made, of one Being with the Father," as the Nicene Creed declares.

But Jesus is also fully human. He isn't some kind of in-between being, a half-God/half-man hybrid. He's both fully and truly divine, and fully and truly human. He's as human as you are. And that means Jesus is not only God-with-us, he's also become us-with-God. He's the true humanity; the true Israel; the true people of God.

~

In the Garden of Eden, the first human being, Adam, faced temptation. He had to choose to trust God or doubt God, to follow God or follow Satan. Humanity in the person of Adam failed the test and sin entered the human race. Now we all have an in-built bias against God. Adam set humanity on a course that ends in destruction (Romans 5 v 12).

So God chose a new people to be his people—the people of Israel. They would be the people through whom he would bless all nations. He gave Israel a new beginning. He rescued them from Egypt and brought them before his throne (symbolised by Mount Sinai) to make a covenant with them. Indeed, God calls the nation his firstborn "son" (Exodus 4 v 22-23). This nation of nobodies was reborn as a new humanity.

Then, like Adam, they experienced a period of testing. They were tempted as they journeyed through the wilderness. They sent twelve spies to investigate the land God had promised them. Ten spies returned with stories of giants, of a people too powerful for the Israelites to defeat. The other two returned with the same stories of giants. But they saw a people the Israelites could defeat with God's help. So the Israelites were presented with a clear choice. They could choose to trust God or doubt God, to take the land or run away. And the new humanity failed the test. As a result, that generation of Israelites spent forty years in the wilderness.

∾

In Luke 3 v 21-22 Jesus is baptised. Like Israel, he passes through the River Jordan en route to inherit the land. Like Israel, he's called God's Son. But Jesus is not just the new Israel; he's also the new humanity. So Luke then traces his genealogy, taking it all the way back to "Adam, the son of God" (Luke 3 v 38).

Then, like Adam and Israel, Jesus is tested by Satan. Like Israel, his testing takes place in the wilderness. Like Israel, it involves 40 units of times: 40 days to parallel their 40 years. Satan tempts Jesus to turn from the task before him. He offers him shortcuts that would compromise his mission. But unlike Adam and unlike Israel, Jesus resists. He is faithful. He is true. Indeed, Jesus responds to Satan's three enticements with three words from the book of Deuteronomy, the record of the words Moses spoke to Israel at the end of their 40 years in the wilderness.

Jesus is the true Adam, trusting God's word. Jesus is the true Israel, remaining faithful to God under pressure in the wilderness. Jesus is the true humanity, perfectly embodying all that humanity was intended to be.

So Jesus is not just the divine Son of God, the second person of the Trinity. Jesus is also the true human son of God, faithful to our Father-Creator. He is the image of God because he perfectly images God as no one but the divine Son could. But he is also the image of God because he perfectly fulfils the calling of humanity to reflect God's glory in God's world, and rule over creation in power and love.

∾

All of this is impressive. It evokes our praise. But on its own it is not really good news. Indeed it's rather intimidating. If Jesus is the model of what it means to be truly human (which he is), then I may as well give up because it's a standard I can never achieve.

But Jesus is also us-with-God. He's our representative. His faithfulness becomes our faithfulness. Our humanity is now wrapped up in his humanity.

We're used to the idea that at Christmas Jesus took on human flesh. He had a real human body. He was flesh and bone. If you cut him, he would bleed. He got sweaty, hungry, tired.

We're also used to the idea that the resurrection of Jesus was a physical resurrection. It's one of the central pillars of our faith. It wasn't just that the memory or ideals of Jesus lived on after his death. He really, literally physically rose from the dead. The risen Christ had a real body, albeit a transformed physical body.

What we don't always appreciate is that the same is true of his ascension. Jesus didn't leave his body behind when he ascended into heaven. It was a real, literal physical ascension. The Jesus who sits at the right hand of God has a real body. He's still as human as you are. There is a human being in the presence of God. He is us-with-God. And he is there as the promise that one day we will join him—along with our resurrected bodies.

∽

What should you do when you're tempted? Look up (with the eyes of faith). Look up and see Jesus in heaven on your behalf. Whatever sin offers can't compare with the glory that awaits you and which is guaranteed for you by the presence of Jesus in heaven.

And what should you do when you fail and fall into temptation? Look up. Look up and see Jesus in heaven as your representative. Your place with God is as secure as his. For Jesus is us-with-God.

Meditate

See what great love the Father has lavished on us, that we should be called children of God! And that is what we are!

(1 John 3 v 1)

Jesus Christ, ascended man,
Passing through the clouds for me,
There before the Father's throne,
Our redeemed humanity.
Human flesh is now with God,
Jesus is our guarantee.

∽

Prayer

Grant, we beseech thee, Almighty God,
that like as we do believe
thy only-begotten Son our Lord Jesus Christ
to have ascended into the heavens;
so we may also in heart and mind thither ascend,
and with him continually dwell,
who liveth and reigneth with thee and the Holy Ghost,
one God, world without end.
Amen.

(The collect for the ascension from the Book of Common Prayer)

The true warrior

*"Come to me, all you who are weary and burdened, and
I will give you rest."*
Matthew 11 v 28

Storyline
Joshua 6

My sisters and I used to sing "Joshua fought the battle of
Jericho" during long car journeys. There are a number
of verses to the song, but I can't remember any lyrics except the
opening lines:

> Joshua fought the battle of Jericho, Jericho, Jericho,
> Joshua fought the battle of Jericho
> and the walls came tumbling down.

So I suspect we sang those lines over and over and over again. The
key line in the song was "and the walls came tumbling down". It was
a good excuse for clapping, shouting and other versions of volume.
I can only imagine that my parents' feelings fluctuated between
relief that we weren't fighting each other and mind-numbing pain
at what can only be described as our repetitive "noise-making".
The irony is that Joshua gave the people of Israel rest. What he gave
my parents was anything but.

It was Joshua who led the people of Israel into the land God had promised to Abraham. And by any calculation his campaign was remarkable. It began with a remarkable escape.

Joshua sent two spies into the land, who were tracked down to the home of Rahab the prostitute. But Rahab switched sides and hid the men on the roof under piles of drying flax. Then she sent the king's soldiers off in the wrong direction before lowering the spies out of window.

Then Joshua led the people through the River Jordan, even though the river was in flood. In the same way that Moses parted the Red Sea, so Joshua parted the river, and the people passed through on dry ground.

Then Joshua defeated the fortress of Jericho (as our song recounts). God told the people to march once round the city for six days and then seven times round on the seventh day. It's hard to know what they thought as they made this bizarre preparation for battle, led, not by the finest warriors, but by the priests. Harder, perhaps, to guess what the inhabitants of the city thought as they watched this spectacle from inside their fortress. Were they amused, bemused or confused? After the final circuit, the trumpets sounded, the people shouted and the walls collapsed. The men were able to enter the city and conquer its people.

There are a couple of glitches in this conquest story. The Israelites were defeated by a small town because one of their number, Achan, had disobeyed God. Then they were deceived by the Gibeonites. But the remarkable victories resumed when Joshua defeated five kings with five armies and God made the sun stand still so Joshua could finish the job. Two major campaigns followed, one capturing the south of the country and the other the north.

The conclusion is this: "The LORD gave them rest on every side, just as he had sworn to their ancestors. Not one of their enemies

withstood them; the LORD gave all their enemies into their hands"
(Joshua 21 v 44). The people could live at peace because their
enemies were defeated.

~

That might have been the end of the story. And you and I might
have found ourselves outside the story and outside this rest. But
there are two reasons why Joshua didn't wrap it all up.

**First, the conclusion to Joshua's story wasn't the full
picture.** Joshua 13 lists the land still be taken, and in Judges 1 – 2 it
becomes clear that the conquest was only partial. Despite the great
start, the people suffered a catastrophic loss of courage (which was
really a loss of faith in God). As a result, the nations they failed to
conquer or drive out remained a thorn in their side.

So Hebrews 4 v 6-7 says:

> *Therefore since it still remains for some to enter that rest, and
> since those who formerly had the good news proclaimed to them
> did not go in because of their disobedience, God again set a
> certain day, calling it "Today".*

In other words, the offer of rest is still open.

Second, God has a bigger agenda. Rest in the land of
Canaan was only a picture of God's ultimate intention. He had
a bigger location in mind—a new creation. And he had a bigger
peace in mind—rest from the ultimate enemies of sin and death.

So Hebrews 4 v 8-9 says:

> *For if Joshua had given them rest, God would not have spoken
> later about another day. There remains, then, a Sabbath-rest for
> the people of God.*

Verse 4 links this rest to the rest of God himself. God invites us not just to peace in Palestine, but to an eternal Sabbath in his presence.

But this requires a new Joshua who will defeat our ultimate enemies: sin and death.

～

When the angel comes to Joseph, he reassures him that the child in Mary's womb has been conceived by the Holy Spirit. Then he says, "You are to give him the name Jesus, because he will save his people from their sins" (Matthew 1 v 21). And "Jesus" is the Greek form of "Joshua". It means "the LORD saves".

Jesus is the new Joshua. He's the ultimate warrior who goes into battle on our behalf. He's the warrior who will "save his people from their sins". He's the warrior who will conquer death.

One day, those who entrust themselves to Jesus will enjoy complete peace. In the new creation there will be no more threats —no accusations, no suffering, no tears. We will share the Sabbath-rest of God with God.

But even now we can enjoy something of that rest. If you feel the need to prove yourself, or control your life, then you'll experience life as frenetic activity. Yet all your endeavour will never seem enough. You'll be like a dog chasing its tail.

That's because we can't prove ourselves—our failures are always there to accuse us. And we can't control our lives or secure our future. No wonder Christmas often feels more of a challenge than a joy.

But Jesus is the new Joshua, come to rescue us from the accusations of sin and set us on course for a secure future. And so Jesus says:

Come to me, all you who are weary and burdened, and I will give you rest. Matthew 11 v 28

If you experience the Christian life as a burden, then something is wrong. You haven't embraced Jesus as your true warrior. You're trying to secure your own future. Don't try to fix this just by taking time off at Christmas. Don't settle for stoic, dutiful service in all the busyness of the Christmas season. Don't settle for a heart that is dull, or anxious or resentful or hopeless. Hear his invitation afresh today:

"Come to me ... and I will give you rest."

∼

Meditate
Come to me, all you who are weary and burdened, and I will give you rest.

We rest on thee, our Shield and our Defender!
We go not forth alone against the foe.
Strong in thy strength, safe in thy keeping tender,
We rest on Thee, and in thy Name we go.

(From "We rest on thee" by Edith Cherry)

Tim Chester

Prayer

Lord Jesus, I pray thee, grant me grace,
that I may never set my heart on the things of this world,
but that all worldly and carnal affections
may utterly die and be mortified in me.
Grant me above all things that I may rest in thee,
and finally quiet and pacify my heart in thee.
For thou, Lord, art the very true peace of heart
and the perfect rest of the soul,
and without thee all things are grievous and unquiet.

Wherefore, Lord Jesus, I pray thee,
give me grace to rest in thee above all things,
and to quiet me in thee above all creatures;
above all glory and honour, above all dignity and power,
above all cunning and policy, above all health and beauty,
above all riches and treasure, above all joy and pleasure,
above all fame and praise, above all mirth and consolation
that man's heart may take or feel besides thee.

For thou, Lord God, art best,
most wise, most high, most mighty,
most sufficient, and most full of all goodness,
most sweet, and most comfortable,
most fair, most loving, most noble, most glorious;
in whom all goodness most perfectly is.
And therefore, whatsoever I have besides thee, it is nothing to me;
for my heart may not rest nor fully be pacified but only in thee.

(A prayer of Catherine Parr, King Henry VIII's sixth wife)

The true judge

"He has performed mighty deeds with his arm;
he has scattered those who are proud
in their inmost thoughts."
Luke 1 v 51-52

Storyline
Judges 13 – 16

I went to our local village fete last weekend. Spread out on the village green was a tea tent serving cream scones, a bric-a-brac stall, a bouncy castle, the local school band, a coconut shy, straw bales for seating, and traditional dancing. All that was missing was Agatha Christie's Miss Marple standing over a corpse.

So it was no surprise to see a "test your strength" stall. You know the sort of thing. You have to hit a target with a mallet and see how high you can send a "mouse". If you send it to the top, then it hits a bell and everyone turns round to see who the local strong man is.

If Samson had been allowed a go, there's no doubt he would have not only hit the bell, but sent it flying.

∽

The people of Israel took possession of the promised land under Joshua's leadership. But a generation after Joshua they got stuck in a loop created by their sin and God's grace. Each generation drifted away from God. So God sent enemies to defeat them. Eventually in their despair the people cried out to God. So God graciously raised up a judge to rescue them. The name "judge" is a bit of misnomer. They were more like warriors who liberated the people. After the judge had defeated their enemy, peace was restored. But then the cycle kicked off all over again as the people drifted away from God.

In some ways Samson was one of the greatest judges. He repeatedly defeated Israel's top enemy of the time, the Philistines. But Samson was also one of the most peculiar judges. In many ways his story mirrors the story of Israel as a whole. All his great exploits begin with his lust.

Samson takes a shine to a Philistine woman and, despite his parents' objections, insists on marrying her. En route to the wedding, he's attacked by a lion. It's an event that leads to one of my favourite lines in the Bible. The Spirit of the LORD came on Samson so that "he tore the lion in pieces as one tears a young goat" (Judges 14 v 6, ESV). I love the way the writer assumes we all know what it's like to tear apart a goat. I think we're supposed to say, "Really? That easily?!" Samson makes a bet with the bride's family when he sets them a riddle. But Samson's bride wheedles the answer out of him and her family wins the bet. Samson has to provide them all with new clothes, which he does by killing 30 Philistines.

Later, Samson goes to collect his new bride, but she's been given to another man. So he catches 300 foxes, ties burning bushes to their tails and lets them loose in the Philistines' fields just before harvest. The Philistines demand justice from the Israelites, so Samson agrees to be handed over to them with his hands bound. But when the

Philistines come to collect him, the Spirit of God again comes upon him. He breaks the ropes as if they are merely charred flax. Then, grabbing the nearest thing to hand, he slaughters a thousand men with the jawbone of a donkey.

On another occasion Samson sleeps with a prostitute. So the Philistines close the gates of the city where he's staying. He's captured. But he merely lifts the gates off their hinges and walks off with the gates on his shoulders.

Finally, Samson falls in love with another Philistine woman—Delilah. The Philistine leaders offer her a small fortune to betray Samson. So she asks Samson the secret of his strength. Three times Samson lies to her and the Philistines fail to capture him. So Delilah says, "How can you say, 'I love you,' when you won't confide in me?" (Judges 16 v 15) The obvious riposte to this is, "And how can you say, 'I love you,' when you keep trying to have me captured?" But it's clear from the stories that Samson can't resist a lady—and so he tells her his secret. If his hair is cut, then he will lose his strength. In a move that everyone but Samson can see a mile off, Delilah has his hair cut while he is asleep, and Samson is overcome, blinded and imprisoned. His story appears to be over.

But God has one last victory planned for Samson. The Philistines are celebrating their triumph in the temple of their god and decide to display the ruined Samson as a symbol of their own strength and power. Samson asks God for one last moment of strength. Pushing on its two central pillars, he brings the whole building down on himself and the Philistine elite. It's estimated that he killed more Philistines in that one act than throughout the rest of his life.

It was when Samson was at his weakest that he achieved his greatest victory. It was through his death that he liberated God's people. *Do you begin to see the echo of the greater story?*

Samson was born to a barren couple after they had been visited by an angel (just as Isaac was). It was, as we saw in chapter seven, part of a pattern that comes to a climax with the birth of Jesus, born to a virgin after she'd been visited by an angel.

Like Samson, Jesus performed many powerful acts throughout his life. He walked on water. He overcame violent men. He cast out demons. He stilled storms. He even raised the dead. Jesus is revealed to be the ultimate "warrior" over sin, disease and death.

But there's a twist. The "campaign" of Jesus ended in defeat. He died the death of a failed revolutionary.

Yet, as with Samson, it was when Jesus was at his weakest that he achieved his greatest victory. His death was no accident. Jesus handed himself over to death. Nor was it really a defeat. For it was through his death that he liberated God's people. He entered into the realm of death to conquer death. He took on death on death's home ground and rose triumphant.

In the song she sings while carrying Jesus in her womb, Mary says:

> *He has performed mighty deeds with his arm;*
> *he has scattered those who are proud in their inmost thoughts.*
> *He has brought down rulers from their thrones*
> *but has lifted up the humble.*   Luke 1 v 51-52

The turn of the year is often a moment when we take stock of the world. In many places oppressive rulers are still on their thrones. But with the coming of the true Judge, we can have absolute confidence that their days are numbered.

∽

Meditate

He has performed mighty deeds with his arm;
he has scattered those who are proud in their inmost thoughts.

And did the Holy and the Just,
The Sovereign of the skies,
Stoop down to wretchedness and dust,
That guilty men might rise?

Yes, the Redeemer left his throne,
His radiant throne on high –
Surprising mercy! Love unknown! –
To suffer, bleed, and die.

(From "And did the Holy and the Just" by Anne Steele)

∾

Prayer

O thou who in almighty power wast weak,
and in perfect excellency wast lowly, grant unto us the same mind.
All that we have which is our own is naught;
if we have any good in us it is wholly thy gift.
O Saviour, since thou, the Lord of heaven and earth,
didst humble thyself, grant unto us true humility,
and make us like thyself;
and then, of thine infinite goodness,
raise us to thine everlasting glory;
who livest and reignest with the Father and the Holy Ghost
for ever and ever. Amen.

(A prayer of Archbishop Thomas Cranmer)

The anointed one

"A shoot will come up from the stump of Jesse;
from his roots a Branch will bear fruit.
The Spirit of the LORD will rest on him—
the Spirit of wisdom and of understanding,
the Spirit of counsel and of might,
the Spirit of the knowledge and fear of the LORD—
and he will delight in the fear of the LORD."
Isaiah 11 v 1-3

Storyline
1 Samuel 16 v 1-14 and Isaiah 11

King Saul stood out from the crowd. Quite literally. When we first meet him in the Bible story, we're told that he was "as handsome a young man as could be found anywhere in Israel, and he was a head taller than anyone else" (1 Samuel 9 v 2). He was head and shoulders above his peers—the obvious choice to be Israel's first king.

The key thing about Israel's judges was not that they were brave and capable, but that the Spirit of God empowered them to lead God's people. And Saul starts off in a similar vein (1 Samuel 10 v 10). He looks like he might be a judge-like king, acting on an as-needs basis with divine power. When Israel is attacked by the Ammonites, Saul leaves his oxen in the fields to lead the rescue (1 Samuel 11). But it soon goes to Saul's head. He decides he doesn't need God's help, and so God rejects him as king.

So God sends the prophet Samuel to the family of Jesse to anoint another king. But who to choose? Easy—the tallest! That's what Samuel assumes. But, no, God has other ideas. Indeed, God's choice isn't even present as Jesse gathers his strapping sons. He's the youngest—literally the "smallest". No one thought he would be needed so he was off on an errand. But, in contrast to tall Saul, it's the smallest who is God's choice. His name is David.

∽

So Samuel took the horn of oil and anointed him in the presence of his brothers, and from that day on the Spirit of the LORD come powerfully upon David.　　　1 Samuel 16 v 13

In the very next verse we read:

Now the Spirit of the LORD had departed from Saul, and an evil spirit from the LORD tormented him.

The Spirit leaves Saul and comes on David.

Israelite kings weren't crowned. They were anointed with oil. So the king was known as "the anointed one". The Hebrew for this is "messiah" and the Greek is "christ". David is the christ (small "c"). He's God's anointed king.

Outwardly, the king was anointed with oil. But what really mattered was being anointed with the Spirit of the LORD. That's what equipped a man to rescue and rule God's people.

David went on to become Israel's greatest king. He defeated

Israel's enemies and gave the people rest in the land. But his successors were not of the same calibre. Even David himself didn't finish well. In the end, the kingdom was lost and David's successors became puppets under Babylonian rule.

∽

And that might have been the end of the story. Isaiah saw this disaster coming. But he also saw beyond it. In a favourite Christmas reading, Isaiah says:

> *A shoot will come up from the stump of Jesse;*
> *from his roots a Branch will bear fruit.*
> *The Spirit of the LORD will rest on him—*
> *the Spirit of wisdom and of understanding,*
> *the Spirit of counsel and of might,*
> *the Spirit of the knowledge and fear of the LORD—*
> *and he will delight in the fear of the LORD.*   Isaiah 11 v 1-3

The house of Jesse, once a strong healthy tree, has been reduced to a stump. But from that stump would come a new King—anointed not with oil, but with the Spirit of the LORD. The Spirit would equip him to rescue and rule God's people. Isaiah goes on to talk about how that king will rule with justice for the poor, how he will bring peace to God's people, and how people from every nation will rally to him. It's almost as if Isaiah imagines Samuel again making that journey to the house of Jesse to anoint a new king.

∽

Samuel was born to a barren woman, Hannah; and Hannah dedicates him to God (1 Samuel 1 v 28). Numbers 6 made provision for a temporary "Nazirite" vow. But Samuel appears to be a permanent Nazirite. Samuel becomes the king-maker who anoints David.

Fast forward to another barren woman, Elizabeth, and another miraculous birth. Elizabeth's son is John the Baptist. And, like Samuel, John appears to be a permanent Nazirite. But if John is the new king-maker, who does he anoint?

One day John is preaching when Jesus appears.

> *When all the people were being baptised, Jesus was baptised too.*
> *And as he was praying, heaven was opened and the Holy Spirit*
> *descended on him in bodily form like a dove. And a voice came*
> *from heaven: "You are my Son, whom I love; with you I am well*
> *pleased."* Luke 3 v 21-22

John's role was to prepare for the coming of God's anointed King. And so it is, with John and Jesus standing together in the River Jordan, that the Spirit anoints Jesus. And the voice from heaven echoes the promise to David of a son who will reign for ever over God's people (2 Samuel 7 v 12-13).

Jesus is anointed by the Spirit to fulfil his role as God's King. Luke tells us Jesus was "full of the Holy Spirit" and "led by the Spirit" (Luke 4 v 1). "Jesus returned to Galilee in the power of the Spirit, and news about him spread through the whole countryside" (v 14). Then Jesus himself says, "The Spirit of the Lord is on me, because he has anointed me to proclaim good news to the poor" (v 18). Jesus is God's anointed One, anointed by the Spirit to rescue and rule God's people.

∾

Even after the resurrection, Luke tells us that Jesus gave instructions *"through the Holy Spirit"* (Acts 1 v 2). But then Jesus says something even more extraordinary.

> *You will receive power when the Holy Spirit comes on you; and*
> *you will be my witnesses in Jerusalem, and in all Judea and*
> *Samaria, and to the ends of the earth.*   Acts 1 v 8

The same Spirit who anointed Jesus comes upon the followers of Jesus. John says we "have anointing from the Holy One" (1 John 2 v 20, 27). In this sense, we are "christs"—anointed royalty because of our connection to the one true King. That doesn't mean we can do everything Jesus did. Jesus was anointed by the Spirit to fulfil the role God had given to him—the unique role of being the Rescuer and Ruler of God's people. We have an anointing from the Holy Spirit to fulfil the role Jesus has given to us—that of being his witnesses to the ends of the earth.

If you don't "feel" that anointing, it might be because you always play safe. This Christmas why not be bold? Speak up and tell someone about Jesus. Open your mouth and expect the Spirit to be at work.

∽

Meditate
The Spirit of the LORD will rest on him—
the Spirit of wisdom and of understanding,
the Spirit of counsel and of might,
the Spirit of the knowledge and fear of the LORD—
and he will delight in the fear of the LORD.

Hail to the Lord's Anointed,
Great David's greater Son!
Hail, in the time appointed,
His reign on earth begun!
He comes to break oppression,
To set the captive free,
To take away transgression,
And rule in equity.

(From "Hail to the Lord's Anointed" by James Montgomery)

∽

Prayer

Breathe on me, breath of God,
Fill me with life anew,
That I may love what thou dost love,
And do what thou wouldst do.

Breathe on me, breath of God,
Until my heart is pure,
Until with thee I will one will,
To do and to endure.

Breathe on me, breath of God,
Blend all my soul with thine,
Until this earthly part of me
Glows with thy fire divine.
Amen.

(From "Breathe on me, breath of God" by Edwin Hatch)

The suffering servant

*"He went and lived in a town called Nazareth.
So was fulfilled what was said through the prophets,
that he would be called a Nazarene."*
Matthew 2 v 23

Storyline
1 Samuel 23 v 7-29 and Isaiah 53

The early Christians had a problem. They proclaimed Jesus as God's King. But what kind of a king comes from Nazareth? What kind of a king not only has no palace, but nowhere at all to lay his head? What kind of king not only has no army, but has instead a motley assortment of unsavoury characters? Jesus just didn't fit the bill.

But that wasn't the half of it. The real problem was this: *What kind of king is crucified?* In Roman society it was impolite even to talk about crucifixion. A Roman citizen couldn't be crucified. It was the ultimate expression of shame. For the Jews, anyone hung on a tree was considered cursed by God. And clearly God's King couldn't be under God's curse.

A suffering king didn't fit the bill. So how did the first Christians overcome these reservations about Jesus?

One solution was to point to the life of David. The early church often quoted from the psalms of David—often psalms from his early life. It suggests they saw the early life of David as a model for Jesus. That's because David didn't actually *become* king when he was anointed by Samuel. After bursting into the public arena with his defeat of Goliath, David very quickly found himself on the wrong side of Saul. As a result he entered his wilderness years. *Literally*. He spent years in the wilderness on the run from Saul, surrounded by a motley assortment of unsavoury characters.

You can imagine the first Christians saying to their Jewish friends, "You say Jesus can't be the promised new David because of his humble life and his early death? But don't you remember the story of David? Don't you remember the sufferings David had to endure? Haven't you sung David's psalms of lament? If Israel's greatest king had to suffer before he came to throne, then why not Israel's ultimate King?"

This appears to be Matthew's point in the odd little episode with which he closed his nativity story:

> *But when [Joseph] heard that Archelaus was reigning in Judea in place of his father Herod, he was afraid to go there. Having been warned in a dream, he withdrew to the district of Galilee, and he went and lived in a town called Nazareth. So was fulfilled what was said through the prophets, that he would be called a Nazarene.* Matthew 2 v 22-23

Here's the problem. Nowhere in the Old Testament does it say the Messiah would be called a Nazarene. Maybe Matthew has in mind Samson, who was a kind of Nazirite, but Jesus doesn't fit the requirements of a Nazirite (he doesn't abstain from wine, for example). More likely, when Matthew uses "Nazarene", he's using a well-known, derogatory slang term for someone coming from an insignificant place like Nazareth in Galilee. That's how Nathanael uses the term when he says, "Nazareth? Can anything good come from there?" (John 1 v 46) "Can God's King be a country bumpkin from Hicksville?" we might say today.

So Matthew doesn't have a specific verse in mind. That's why he talks about "the prophets" (plural) rather than a specific, named prophet. He's alluding to the theme in the story of Israel, especially in the story of David, that God's King will come from "Nowhere-town".

Instead of undermining his claims, the humble origins of Jesus actually reinforce his claims to be God's anointed King.

∼

Another solution to the problem of a suffering King was to point to the prophet Isaiah, who speaks of a suffering servant of the LORD. Isaiah records four "songs" which are sung about a servant or by a servant (42 v 1-4; 49 v 1-7; 50 v 4-10 and 52 v 13 – 53 v 12). Sometimes the servant appears to be Israel, called by God to be a light to the nations. Sometimes the servant appears to be an individual who restores Israel.

What the early church realised is that Jesus is that servant. Jesus is Israel as Israel was meant to be. He is the true people of God. He is the one who lives in perfect obedience to God so that he's the light of the world. But Jesus is also the one who rescues God's people as they are, mired in sin and facing God's judgment. He restores God's people and sets us back on track.

Matthew quotes the first Servant Song in its entirety in Matthew 12 v 18-21. The evidence of Jesus' miracles clearly points to him being the servant of the LORD.

The key thing is that the servant is a *suffering* servant. This is made explicit in the final and most famous song: "He was despised and rejected by mankind," says Isaiah (Isaiah 53 v 3). The rejection of Jesus actually confirms his identity as God's Servant.

But the point is not just that the servant *suffers*. The point is that the servant *rescues* God's people by suffering in their place. His sufferings are not accidental or incidental. They're central to his mission.

> *Surely he took up our pain*
> *and bore our suffering,*
> *yet we considered him punished by God,*
> *stricken by him, and afflicted.*
> *But he was pierced for our transgressions,*
> *he was crushed for our iniquities;*
> *the punishment that brought us peace was on him,*
> *and by his wounds we are healed.*
> *We all, like sheep, have gone astray,*
> *each of us has turned to our own way;*
> *and the LORD has laid on him*
> *the iniquity of us all.* Isaiah 53 v 4-6

The crucifixion was not a sad anti-climax to a promising start. It was the crowning glory of the King's mission.

∽

Christmas in our culture is about presents and parties, family and food. In the process, Jesus is often pushed to the margins at his own birthday celebrations! There's nothing new in this. Jesus has always been marginalised by our world. But it doesn't mean he's not real. And it doesn't mean he's not returning as the King of the world.

Meditate

But he was pierced for our transgressions,
he was crushed for our iniquities.

(Isaiah 53 v 5)

He came from his blest throne salvation to bestow;
But men made strange, and none
The longed-for Christ would know:
But O, my Friend, my Friend indeed,
Who at my need his life did spend.

Sometimes they strew his way, and his sweet praises sing,
Resounding all the day
Hosannas to their King.
Then "Crucify!" is all their breath,
And for his death they thirst and cry.

They rise and needs will have my dear Lord made away.
A murderer they save,
The Prince of life they slay.
Yet cheerful he to suffering goes,
That he his foes from thence might free.

In life no house, no home, my Lord on earth might have.
In death no friendly tomb,
But what a stranger gave.
What may I say? Heav'n was his home,
But mine the tomb wherein he lay.

(From "My song is love unknown" by Samuel Crossman)

Prayer

The gift of thy only-begotten Son Jesus Christ our Lord,
who thou gavest unto us
to be our Saviour, our Redeemer, our Peace-maker,
our Wisdom, our Sanctification, and our Righteousness,
is the most excellent gift and most precious treasure!

Wonderfully, O most loving Father,
doth this thing set forth thy hearty love toward us,
that when we were yet ungodly and wicked sinners,
thou gavest thy Son to die for our sins.
Amen

(Thomas Becon)

The ultimate king

"He will be great and will be called the Son of the Most High. The Lord God will give him the throne of his father David, and he will reign over Jacob's descendants for ever; his kingdom will never end."

Luke 1 v 32-33

Storyline

2 Samuel 7 – 8; 2 Kings 18 – 19 and 2 Kings 22 – 23

One of the most enduring British legends is that of King Arthur. We love the stories of the sword from the stone, the quest for the holy grail, and the partnership with Merlin. We love the tales of the knights of the round table: their exploits, their courage, their honour. And then there is the promise that Arthur will return when the nation is under threat. A few good contenders for moments of national peril have come and gone with no sign of Arthur. So perhaps we shouldn't bank too much on him turning up.

A similar expectation grew in Israel around the rather more historical figure of King David—only this expectation was backed up by the firm and sure promise of God.

'The LORD gave David victory wherever he went" (2 Samuel 8 v 6, 14). The defeat of Goliath is perhaps David's most famous victory. But 2 Samuel 8 lists a host of other victories. As a result the Lord gave David and the people "rest from all his enemies around him" (2 Samuel 7 v 1). But it was short-lived. David's own sin threw the country into a horrific and bloody civil war.

David offered to *build a house for God*—a temple of stone to replace the cloth tabernacle. But instead, God promised to *build a house for David*—in the sense of a dynasty. But then David committed adultery with Bathsheba. When she fell pregnant, David arranged the murder of her husband, Uriah. But the cover-up did not evade God's attention. God said that the sword would never leave David's house—his family. Not long afterwards, one of David's sons raped his half-sister, Tamar (2 Samuel 13). David lost the moral authority to rule his family. So another son, Absalom, exacted revenge. Then Absalom deposed his father for a time (2 Samuel 14 – 19).

Things didn't improve with the next generation. Solomon started well, but he married foreign wives and worshipped foreign gods. He also enslaved the people. As a result, when Solomon's son came to the throne, the ten northern tribes rebelled and the kingdom was divided.

With a few exceptions, the trajectory from David onwards was firmly set in a downwards direction. Successive kings in both the northern kingdom of Israel and the southern kingdom of Judah did not follow God and led the people astray. And so the expectation grew, fuelled by God's prophets, that God would send a new King David—an ultimate Messiah or Christ. This King would rescue Israel from her enemies, rule in justice and make her a light to the nations.

∾

King Hezekiah looked as if he might fit the bill. "He did what was right in the eyes of the LORD, just as his father David had done" (2 Kings 18 v 3). He removed the idolatrous altars from the nation and refused to submit to Assyria, the superpower of the day. So the Assyrian army arrived outside Jerusalem to teach him a lesson. The king of Assyria sent Hezekiah a letter reminding him that plenty of other nations had thought their god would save them, but they had all been destroyed by the Assyrians. Why did Hezekiah think he would be any different?

What would you do? Hezekiah took the letter, laid it out in the temple and prayed to God. In essence he said, *It's your reputation that's at stake, LORD.* The next morning the Israelites woke up to find 185,000 Assyrian corpses, killed by an angel of the LORD.

"Hezekiah trusted in the LORD the God of Israel," comments the writer of Kings.

> *There was no one like him among all the kings of Judah, either*
> *before him or after him. He held fast to the LORD and did*
> *not stop following him … he was successful in whatever he*
> *undertook.*   2 Kings 18 v 5-7

It's hard to imagine a better commendation than that.

But Hezekiah was not the new David. Despite a 15-year postponement, his life ended in death. Indeed, in later life he made the mistake of showing off his treasures to visiting Babylonians. The Babylonians didn't forget, and a few generations later they returned to help themselves.

∾

King Josiah was another good contender for the role of "new David". He was only eight when he came to the throne. But right from the start...

> *he did what was right in the eyes of the LORD and followed*
> *completely the ways of his father David, not turning aside to the*
> *right or to the left.* 2 Kings 22 v 2

Josiah initiated a renovation of the temple during which they found a lost copy of the Book of the Law. When Josiah realised how far the nation was off track, he called for national repentance and covenant renewal. Maybe Josiah would be a new David? But no, Josiah died at the hands of an Egyptian army in a foolhardy intervention in a conflict that wasn't even his problem.

When the line of David was deposed and the people carried off into exile, it looked as if the hopes of a new David to re-establish a golden era had come to an end.

∽

But several hundred years later, an angel told Mary she would conceive through the Holy Spirit. This is what the angel said about the son to whom Mary would give birth:

> *He will be great and will be called the Son of the Most High.*
> *The Lord God will give him the throne of his father David, and*
> *he will reign over Jacob's descendants for ever; his kingdom will*
> *never end.* Luke 1 v 32-33

Nine months later shepherds were out in the hills when they, too, encountered an angel. The angel says:

Do not be afraid. I bring you good news that will cause great joy for all the people. Today in the town of David a Saviour has been born to you; he is the Messiah, the Lord. Luke 2 v 10-11

The story of all Israel's kings from David onwards comes to its climax in the birth of Jesus. Jesus is son of David, the ultimate David, the promised Messiah.

"Hezekiah ... held fast to the LORD." Like David, Hezekiah and Josiah, Jesus would hold fast to God. But Jesus wouldn't have the flaws that ultimately undermined the reigns of his predecessors. His reign would be "good news" and would "cause great joy for all the people".

"The LORD gave David victory wherever he went." Like David, Hezekiah and Josiah, God would give Jesus victory. But Jesus would go further. He would take on death and God would give him victory over death. So his kingdom will never end.

Meditate

He will be great and will be called the Son of the Most High.

Look, ye saints, the sight is glorious,
See the Man of Sorrows now,
From the fight returned victorious,
Every knee to him shall bow.
Crown him! Crown him!
Crowns become the Victor's brow.

(From "Look, ye saints, the sight is glorious" by Thomas Kelly)

Prayer

*Grant that I may ever desire and will
that which is most pleasant and most acceptable to thee.
Thy will be my will, and my will be to follow alway thy will.
Let there be alway in me one will, and one desire with thee;
and that I have no desire to will or not to will, but as thou wilt.
Lord, thou knowest what thing is most profitable
and most expedient for me.
Give, therefore, what thou wilt, as much as thou wilt, and when thou wilt.
Do with me what thou wilt, as it shall please thee,
and shall be most to thine honour.
Put me where thou wilt, and freely do with me in all things after thy will.
Thy creature I am, and in thy hands, lead and turn me where thou wilt.
Lo, I am thy servant, ready to do all things that thou commandest;
for I desire not to live to myself, but to thee.
Amen.*

(A prayer of Catherine Parr, King Henry VIII's sixth wife)

The good shepherd

"I, the shepherd, have done wrong.
These are but sheep. What have they done?
Let your hand fall on me and my family."
2 Samuel 24 v 17

Storyline
Genesis 22 and 2 Samuel 24

D o you have any regrets? Have you ever done something and then immediately realised it was wrong? No sooner were the words out of your mouth than you wished you could take them back? Of course you have. You're human. Perhaps this Christmas you're dreading meeting up with a family member or an old friend because you know you ought to say sorry to them. But what if you've wronged the God who rules the universe? *What happens then?*

∽

The story of David's reign as told in 1 and 2 Samuel ends in regret. At first sight it appears a rather odd finale. With so many high points to choose from, the writer ends the narrative on a downbeat note with one of David's failures. Plus it's the story of a census—an act of bureaucracy. But it's not the anti-climax it first appears to be.

David ordered a count of all the fighting men in Judah. It was the wrong thing to do. Joab, David's commander, knew it. David realised it almost as soon as it was complete. We, however, are not told *why* it was wrong. After all, God himself had initiated a census in Numbers 1 (hence the name of the book). Perhaps it was an act of misplaced self-confidence. But perhaps, too, there's a clue in the outcome—a plague. It's the term used to describe the judgments that fell on Egypt when Egypt enslaved God's people. Perhaps David had forced labour in mind when he ordered the census. Whatever the reason:

> *David was conscience-stricken after he had counted the fighting men, and he said to the LORD, "I have sinned greatly in what I have done. Now, LORD, I beg you, take away the guilt of your servant. I have done a very foolish thing."* 2 Samuel 24 v 10

The prophet Gad gives David three options: three years of famine, three months of fleeing from their enemies or three days of plague. David answers, "Let us fall into the hands of the LORD, for his mercy is great; but do not let me fall into human hands" (v 14). Judgment will be done, but David chooses judgment directly from God rather than indirectly from human beings. For David knows that God's judgment is never excessive and is often tinged with mercy.

An angel sent by God brings plague across the nation. Seventy-thousand people die. The angel is then poised to bring disaster on the capital, Jerusalem. I imagine it as a dark cloud hanging over the city. But at the last minute God relents and tells the angel to withdraw. David's confidence in God's mercy has been justified.

So the angel's onslaught halts at the threshing floor of Araunah the Jebusite. The prophet Gad tells David to build an altar on the site. Justice must be done. Wrong must be put right. Judgment must fall. But the sacrificial animals will symbolically die in the place of the people. The animals will bear the punishment of death that the people deserve.

2 Chronicles 3 v 1 tells us that the threshing floor of Araunah was located on Mount Moriah, the very spot where a thousand years before, Abraham had offered his son, Isaac, at God's command. It was a test of Abraham's faith in God's power to bring life from death (not that Abraham knew that beforehand). But again at the last minute, God intervened. God provided a ram to die in the place of Isaac.

But that's not all. 2 Chronicles 3 v 1 also tells us that the threshing floor of Araunah was the place where Solomon built the temple. This spot became the permanent place of sacrifice.

∼

But there's a problem. The sacrifice of animals was only ever a *symbol*. The death of animals couldn't really sort out the problem of human sin. It was a picture or promise of the atonement that God would provide. *But from where would that come?*

In 2 Samuel 24 v 17, as David sees the angel striking down his people, he says to God:

I have sinned; I, the shepherd, have done wrong.
These are but sheep. What have they done?
Let your hand fall on me and my family.

David offers *himself* as the one to make atonement. He invites God to lay the guilt of the people on his family. He describes himself as "the shepherd", who should take responsibility for his flock.

～

A thousand years later the coming of the Magi from the East prompts a search of the Scriptures by the religious leaders on Herod's behalf. They discover a promise in Micah 5 v 2-4:

> *But you, Bethlehem, in the land of Judah,*
> *are by no means least among the rulers of Judah;*
> *for out of you will come a ruler*
> *who will shepherd my people Israel.*   Matthew 2 v 6

The baby in the manger will be the shepherd who takes responsibility for God's people. Jesus owns the title and the role for himself when he declares:

> *I am the good shepherd. The good shepherd lays down his life for*
> *the sheep.*   John 10 v 11

And the baby in the manger is the son of David. The unresolved judgment that hangs over David's family will fall on Jesus. Jesus is the one who will make atonement for the people.

And so it was. Jesus was crucified not far from the temple, not far from the threshing floor of Araunah, and not far from Mount Moriah. But this time there was no last-minute intervention or substitute. Jesus himself is the substitute. He is the sacrifice. He is the one who atones for our guilt and averts God's judgment.

～

You might want to think about your regrets. Perhaps there are people to whom you need to say sorry. Christmas time is a great opportunity to do this. Use some of your time off to reflect and pray. Send Christmas cards or messages to those you have become distant from, for whatever reason. Arrange to meet up.

And what about the wrong you've done to God? Perhaps it's time to say sorry to God as well. And to think about what God needs to change in you in the year ahead.

∽

Meditate

"Lord, I beg you, take away the guilt of your servant.
I have done a very foolish thing."

(2 Samuel 24 v 10)

From east to west, from shore to shore,
Let ev'ry heart awake and sing:
The holy child whom Mary bore,
The Christ, the everlasting king.

Behold, the world's Creator wears
The form and fashion of a slave.
Our very flesh our maker shares,
His fallen creatures all to save.

(Coelius Sedulius, trans. John Ellerton)

∽

Prayer

O most loving Father, weigh not my sins,
but remember the most gentle promises.
Consider not my evil works,
but have respect unto the undefiled deeds of thy Son Jesus Christ,
whom thou hast given to be my Redeemer, my Saviour,
my righteousness, my atonement-maker, my satisfaction,
and the alone and all wholly sufficient sacrifice for my sins.
For his sake, for his innocency and righteousness,
have mercy on me, O God, according to thy great mercy,
and put away all my unrighteousness for thy tender compassion.
I have gone astray like a sheep that was lost:
yet, O Lord, for thy mercy's sake, seek me up,
lay me upon thy shoulders,
and bring me home again to thy sheepfold.
Amen.

(Thomas Becon)

The wisdom of God

*"And the child grew and became strong;
he was filled with wisdom,
and the grace of God was on him."*

Luke 2 v 40

Storyline

1 Kings 3 and 1 Corinthians 1 v 18-31

"What do you want for Christmas?" It's what countless parents ask their children as the day approaches. "A pony? Maybe not as a big as a pony—we're not made of money." Children soon learn there's an unofficial scale and start to pitch their requests accordingly.

But imagine you could have anything you wanted? Imagine the giver had unlimited resources.

Not long after Solomon becomes king, God appears to him in a dream. "Ask for whatever you want me to give you," he says (1 Kings 3 v 5). Whatever you want! Victory? Wealth? Lands? Power? Adulation? Solomon asks for something different:

Now, LORD my God, you have made your servant king in place of my father David. But I am only a little child and do not

> *know how to carry out my duties. Your servant is here among the*
> *people you have chosen, a great people, too numerous to count or*
> *number. So give your servant a discerning heart to govern your*
> *people and to distinguish between right and wrong. For who is*
> *able to govern this great people of yours?* 1 Kings 3 v 7-9

Not long after, Solomon's wisdom is put to the test. Two prostitutes come to him. Both have recently given birth, but one child has died. Now one of the prostitutes claims the other has switched the corpse for her living child. But the other claims the living child belongs to her. Who can decide between these rival claims? Solomon's famous solution is to order that the baby be cut in two—they can have half each. This seems fair to one of the mothers. The other is horrified and immediately drops her suit to save the child. Solomon orders the baby to be given to her—she's the genuine mother for she genuinely cares for the child.

It's not just Solomon who is wise. Under his reign Israel experiences an intellectual and cultural renaissance. Poetry, songs and literature are all written, some of which we have in our Bibles. Solomon's fame spreads far and wide.

> *From all nations people came to listen to Solomon's wisdom, sent*
> *by all the kings of the world, who had heard of his wisdom.*
>
> 1 Kings 4 v 34

The top celebrity visitor was the Queen of Sheba, who arrived with a camel train of treasures and left impressed. "Because of the LORD's eternal love for Israel," she told Solomon, "he has made you king to maintain justice and righteousness" (1 Kings 10 v 9).

∾

We often talk about the "three wise men" who visited the infant Jesus. But we're not told how many there were (only that they brought three gifts), and they're described as "Magi"—from which we get the word "magician". Most probably they were astrologers. No, if we want to find a wise person in the nativity story, then we need to look into the manger, not around it. Paul says that Jesus "has become for us wisdom from God" (1 Corinthians 1 v 30). Ultimate wisdom is found in the person of Jesus.

Does this mean that the baby Jesus was very clever? No, though his understanding of the Scriptures, even as a child, was amazing (Luke 2 v 47), and his ability to read people's hearts was supernatural.

To understand how Jesus is our wisdom we need to go back to Solomon, who said, "The fear of the LORD is the beginning of knowledge" (Proverbs 1 v 7).

The main problem we face in understanding God, ourselves and the world around us is not an intellectual one. Our main problem is that our thinking is distorted by our pride and selfishness. We are adept at finding reasons to justify what we want to do. You'll know how this works if you've ever talked through a decision with someone who's already made up their mind. They find reasons for rejecting other options and make the most of supporting arguments. The reality is that *we all do this all the time* to justify our independence from God.

This is why the beginning of knowledge, or wisdom, is the fear of the LORD. More important than having a degree or being well-read or having access to Google is submission to God. We submit our wills to him so we acknowledge his rule. And we submit our pride to him so we acknowledge our need.

This is where Jesus comes in. Jesus turns the wisdom of the world upside down. Those who are self-willed and self-reliant will only ever see the cross as weakness and folly.

> *Jews demand signs and Greeks look for wisdom, but we preach Christ crucified: a stumbling-block to Jews and foolishness to Gentiles, but to those whom God has called, both Jews and Greeks, Christ the power of God and the wisdom of God. For the foolishness of God is wiser than human wisdom, and the weakness of God is stronger than human strength.*
>
> 1 Corinthians 1 v 22-25

God has chosen to reveal himself in a form that the proud will never recognise. But when God opens our eyes, we are able to see in Christ true *"wisdom from God—that is, our righteousness, holiness and redemption"* (v 30).

∾

So what do you want for Christmas this year? What would you ask God for?

We've already been given the gift that Solomon asked for. We've been given wisdom in the person of Jesus. Jesus is the one who leads us to reliable hope and to lasting happiness. He provides a sure guide for the complexities of life. The key thing is to come to him acknowledging his rule and acknowledging our need. Then you'll make wise decisions. The question is not whether God will give you wisdom. The question is whether you'll receive it.

∾

Meditate

The fear of the LORD *is the beginning of knowledge.*

(Proverbs 1 v 7)

O come, Thou Wisdom from on high,
And order all things, far and nigh.
To us the path of knowledge show,
And cause us in her ways to go.
Rejoice! Rejoice! Immanuel
Shall come to thee, O Israel.

(From the 12th-century Latin hymn, "O come, O come, Immanuel',
translated by H. S. Coffin)

∽

Prayer

O Lord, heavenly Father,
in whom is the fulness of light and wisdom,
enlighten our minds by thy Holy Spirit,
and give us grace to receive thy word
with reverence and humility,
without which no man can understand thy truth,
for Christ's sake.
Amen.

(John Calvin)

The whisper of God

Storyline
1 Kings 18 v 16 – 19 v 18

What would you like God to do in your neighbourhood or family or nation? Tear through your neighbourhood with great power? Shake things up in your family? Purge the nation of evil? The prophet Elijah would have settled for any of those options. But what he got was a gentle whisper and a question.

∼

Elijah's contest at Mount Carmel is one of the highpoints of the Bible story. Elijah challenges the prophets of Baal to a contest. Both will ask their God to send down fire on an altar. The prophets of Baal get nowhere. Then it's Eljiah's turn. But first he makes things harder for himself by having his altar drenched in water, just so there can be no doubt about what is to follow. When he prays,

God answers with fire. The LORD wins hands down and the people execute the prophets of Baal.

But just when Elijah thinks he's carried the day, he gets a message from Queen Jezebel threatening his death (1 Kings 19 v 2). Elijah hits the road. Is he running in fear? Or is he after a showdown with God? His reasons are not made clear to us, but either way he ends up at Mount Horeb.

> *The LORD said, "Go out and stand on the mountain in the presence of the LORD, for the LORD is about to pass by." Then a great and powerful wind tore the mountains apart and shattered the rocks before the LORD, but the LORD was not in the wind. After the wind there was an earthquake, but the LORD was not in the earthquake. After the earthquake came a fire, but the LORD was not in the fire. And after the fire came a gentle whisper. When Elijah heard it, he pulled his cloak over his face and went out and stood at the mouth of the cave.*

1 Kings 19 v 11-13

Baal was a nature god. But the true God is very different. He can send a wind or earthquake or fire. But he's not a wind or an earthquake or a fire. He's not *in* nature. He's *above* nature. He's not some impersonal force we encounter in creation's beauty or power. God is a *personal* God. He's three persons: Father, Son and Spirit, living in eternal community and open to community with us. That's the point of the gentle whisper. God speaks. Winds don't speak. Only persons speak.

God tears apart mountains and shatters rocks in verse 11. But with Elijah nursing his bruises, God is gentle—as gentle as a whisper. He comes near through his word to restore Elijah's soul.

∽

Twice God asks, "What are you doing here, Elijah?" (v 9, 13) Why has Elijah come to Mount Horeb—or Mount Sinai as it's better known? Let's recap. This is what had previously happened at Mount Sinai:

> *Mount Sinai was covered with smoke, because the LORD*
> *descended on it in fire. The smoke billowed up from it like smoke*
> *from a furnace, and the whole mountain trembled violently.*
>
> Exodus 19 v 18

Now God has recreated this moment for Elijah.

At Mount Sinai, Moses had asked to see God's glory. So God said he would "pass by" and proclaim his name (Exodus 33 v 19, 22). Now he uses the same expression with Elijah (1 Kings 19 v 11). Moreover verse 9 literally says God brought Elijah to "the cave"—the cave on the mountain where God hid Moses to show his glory and reveal his Name:

> *The LORD, the LORD, the compassionate and gracious God,*
> *slow to anger, abounding in love and faithfulness...*
>
> Exodus 34 v 6

The revelation of God's glory was not in the might of the wind or fire. It was in the gentle whisper of his Name. *"Compassionate and gracious ... slow to anger, abounding in love."* This is the true glory of God.

∽

God tells Elijah to anoint Hazael, Jehu and Elisha. Hazael and Jehu will be instruments of divine judgment. Israel as a nation will die. And *"yet"* (v 18), God will save a remnant, the seeds of a new beginning. The nation will be reborn.

In Elijah's day, there were just 7,000 who were faithful to God. At other stages of Israel's history, there may have been many fewer. And in the end, the faithful people of God came down to just one single person—Jesus. All his disciples abandoned him and he alone was left. Then he died and the faithful people of God died with him. There was no one left.

But three days later he rose again. And we rise with him. The people of God are reborn.

God triumphs through a faint whisper. God himself in the person of his Son hangs on a Roman cross. The weight of his body would have made breathing difficult. His mouth is dry. Every breath is a struggle. Then, in what must have been the faintest of whispers, he says, *"It is finished"* (John 19 v 30). To the world it is the finish of a life. But Jesus is declaring the finish of a plan. This is God's victory. This is God's glory. This dying whisper is the ultimate revelation of God. This is how God is known.

It's at the cross that we see "The LORD, the LORD, the compassionate and gracious God, slow to anger, abounding in love and faithfulness…"

∽

Maybe Elijah was hoping for "a great and powerful wind" to tear through Israel to shatter God's enemies. But God was not in the wind. Maybe Elijah was hoping for an earthquake to shake things up and usher in a new regime. But God was not in the earthquake. Maybe Elijah was hoping for a fire to purge God's people. But God was not in the fire.

Instead Elijah got a gentle whisper and a question: "What are you doing here?" God makes himself known not through winds, quakes or fire, but through the testimony of 7,000 people, some hiding in caves (18 v 4; 19 v 18).

If Elijah wants to see God at work, then he must return from Sinai to the chaos and threat of messy life in Israel, and lift up his voice, however faint and lonely it may seem.

How will God reveal himself in your neighbourhood? Through a gentle whisper. Through *your* gentle whisper of gospel hope in the death and resurrection of Jesus. How could you get started with that this Christmas?

∽

Meditate

What are you doing here?

(1 Kings 18 v 9, 13)

O Word of God incarnate,
O Wisdom from on high,
O Truth unchanged, unchanging,
O Light of our dark sky:
We praise you for the radiance
That from the Scripture's page,
A lantern to our footsteps,
Shines on from age to age.

(From "O Word of God incarnate" by William Walsham How)

∽

Prayer

O heavenly Father,
the author and fountain of all truth,
the bottomless sea of all understanding,
send, we beseech thee, thy Holy Spirit into our hearts,
and lighten our understandings
with the beams of thy heavenly grace.
We ask this, O merciful Father,
for the sake of thy dear Son, our Saviour, Jesus Christ.
Amen.

(Bishop Nicholas Ridley)

The presence of God

21

*"Therefore the Lord himself will give you a sign:
the virgin will conceive and give birth to a son,
and will call him Immanuel."*
Isaiah 7 v 14

Storyline
Isaiah 7

Keep calm and carry on. Those words were printed on posters in a now iconic font to motivate Britons during World War Two. Very few posters were actually displayed. But an old copy was discovered in 2000, and since then "Keep calm" products (and ironic variations) have proliferated. Perhaps you'll find a "Keep calm" mug in your stocking. Perhaps you'll need that reminder at some point over the Christmas period!

"Keep calm and carry on" is pretty much the prophet Isaiah's message to King Ahaz.

"Keep calm and don't be afraid," were his precise words (7 v 4).

∽

King Ahaz is the king of Judah and a descendant of David. But he's not like his forefather. He's capitulated to the culture of the surrounding nations. He's even sacrificed his children. The story of Ahaz is going to be a turning point in the line of David.

The kings of Aram and Israel (sometimes known as "Ephraim") have formed an alliance and invaded Judah (v 1-2). So the prophet Isaiah meets Ahaz at the upper pool—probably part of the preparations for a siege—and calls on him to trust in God. If Ahaz trusts in God, then God will deliver him (v 3-7). But if Ahaz looks elsewhere—and that means making an alliance with Assyria, the rising superpower of the day—then he'll fail and fall (v 8-10). Ahaz must choose: trust in God and his promises or trust in Assyria and their military power.

God goes further: "Ask the LORD your God for a sign, whether in the deepest depths or in the highest heights" (v 11). In other words, God promises to move heaven and hell to rescue Ahaz if Ahaz turns to him. Ahaz's reply sounds pious—"I will not put the LORD to the test". But in reality he's saying, "I don't need a sign because I've already made up my mind—I'm making an alliance with Assyria".

So God gives Ahaz an unwanted sign:

> *Therefore the Lord himself will give you a sign: the virgin will conceive and give birth to a son, and will call him Immanuel.*
>
> Isaiah 7 v 14

Suddenly this story of kings, war and international politics gets all Christmassy! But for Ahaz this sign isn't good news. What it indicates is that God will bring the reign of the house of David to an end. Instead, God will raise up a new king from a virgin.

> *The LORD will bring on you and on your people and on the house of your father a time unlike any since Ephraim broke away from Judah—he will bring the king of Assyria.* v 17

King Ahaz will get Assyria as he wants, but Assyria will come to destroy him rather than rescue him. Ultimately the failure of this king of the house of David will lead to defeat and exile (v 18-25).

But God remains faithful to his promise to David. The reign of the house of David will end, but *the line of David* will continue. The curious reference to "a virgin" suggests something strange. A break in the line—the need for a new kind of king. Ahaz thinks he can manage without God. But it's God who can manage without Ahaz. God can raise up a king from a virgin.

∽

The events which Isaiah predicted came true. The kings of Aram and Israel fell to the Assyrian onslaught. But then the Assyrians subjugated Judah. In time, Judah went into exile under the Babylonians. The collapse of the rule of the king of David's line meant the end of the symbols of God's presence: the temple was destroyed and the people were exiled from the land.

But there is hope. Isaiah promises that God will once again be present with his people. He will be present through the promised child for the child's name will be "Immanuel", which means "God with us". And the name of Isaiah's son, Shear-jashub, means "a remnant shall return" (7 v 3). God will come to his people and lead them home. This section of Isaiah comes to a climax in 9 v 1-7:

> *There will be no more gloom for those who were in distress.*
> *In the past he humbled the land of Zebulun and the land of*
> *Naphtali, but in the future he will honour Galilee of the nations,*
> *by the Way of the Sea, beyond the Jordan—*
>
> *The people walking in darkness have seen a great light;*
> *on those living in the land of deep darkness a light has dawned ...*

> *For to us a child is born, to us a son is given,*
> *and the government will be on his shoulders.*
> *And he will be called Wonderful Counsellor, Mighty God,*
> *Everlasting Father, Prince of Peace.*
> *Of the greatness of his government and peace there will be no end.*
> *He will reign on David's throne and over his kingdom,*
> *establishing and upholding it with justice and righteousness*
> *from that time on and for ever.*
> *The zeal of the LORD Almighty will accomplish this.*

Matthew says this promised son is the son who was born to the virgin in Bethlehem. The birth of a boy to a virgin took place, he says, "to fulfil what the Lord had said through the prophet" (Matthew 1 v 22-23). He goes on to quote Isaiah 9 in Matthew 4 v 15-16 to describe the ministry of Jesus is Galilee. As Isaiah promised, Galilee sees the first rays of the dawning salvation as Jesus begins his ministry there.

The baby in the manger is Immanuel. God is going to re-establish his rule through this child. God is going to restore his people, rescuing us from sin and judgment.

∽

What should we do? We should do what Ahaz should have done: *"Keep calm and don't be afraid. Do not lose heart."* Ahaz should have found confidence in the word of God. He should have trusted the promise of a Saviour. And so should we.

Maybe you're tempted to lose heart when you see people ignoring God or mocking God. We need to trust God's promises that Christ will be vindicated. Otherwise we'll despair and gradually align ourselves with the rebellious majority. Keep calm and don't lose heart.

Or maybe your challenges are a little more domestic. You're flustered because you're trying to secure your future. You're unsettled because you are unsure about what will happen next with your family or your job. You're agitated because you're desperate to keep everyone happy this Christmas. Jesus invites us to look at life from a heavenly perspective and realign our priorities. Then some of the things that make us panic don't seem quite so important. And for things that remain important, we can tell ourselves: God's King reigns for ever—*keep calm and don't lose heart.*

∽

Meditate

And he will be called Wonderful Counsellor, Mighty God,
Everlasting Father, Prince of Peace.
Of the greatness of his government and peace there will be no end.

(Isaiah 9 v 6-7)

Bright and joyful is the morn, unto us a child is born.
From the highest realms of heaven unto us a son is given.

On his shoulder he shall bear power and majesty, and wear
On his vesture and his thigh, names most awful, names most high.

Wonderful in counsel he, the incarnate deity,
Sire of ages, ne'er to cease, King of kings and Prince of Peace.

Come and worship at his feet, yield to Christ the homage meet.
From his manger to his throne, homage due to God alone.

(Traditional Sheffield carol)

Tim Chester

Prayer

Lord, I believe;

help thou mine unbelief.

Amen.

(Mark 9 v 24, Authorised Version)

The end of exile

*"The beginning of the good news about Jesus
the Messiah, the Son of God, as it is written in
Isaiah the prophet ... 'a voice of one calling in the
wilderness, "Prepare the way for the Lord, make straight
paths for him."'"*
Mark 1 v 1, 3

Storyline
Ezra 1 and Nehemiah 1

Home. For some people it's a place of boredom. For some it's a place of threat. But for most of us home is a place of security, welcome, familiarity. We love coming home. For the Jewish exiles home evoked painful feelings of longing and regret. "By the rivers of Babylon we sat and wept when we remembered Zion" (Psalm 137 v 1).

Both the northern kingdom of Israel and the southern kingdom of Judah ended up in exile. This was the ultimate curse which God had warned would fall on those who broke his covenant (see Deuteronomy 28 v 64).

But what happened to Israel was a microcosm of humanity's experience. When Adam and Eve rebelled against God, they were exiled from the Garden of Eden. The way home was barred by an angel with a flaming sword. We live our lives cut off from God.

Who can lead us home?

∽

For the Jewish exiles in Babylon it looked as if Ezra might be the man. The Babylonians had defeated Judah and led the nation into exile. But 70 years later the Babylonians were themselves defeated by the Persians, and the opportunity arose to return. Ezra led the first wave. But it was not straightforward. The temple was in ruins and Jerusalem—what was left of it—was undefended. Plus the neighbours weren't happy.

Back in Persia Nehemiah gets a report from his brother. Nehemiah is a Jew with an important role in the Persian court. But when he hears of the troubles back home, he gets permission to make a visit to Jerusalem. Perhaps Nehemiah is the man to end the exile.

Nehemiah finds the wall of Jerusalem in a poor state. So he organises its reconstruction. The neighbouring nations are unimpressed so they start insulting and threatening the project. The workers are forced to take turns to build the wall and stand guard, swords in hand. It wasn't just the wall Nehemiah wanted to restore. He stamped out the oppression of the poor among the Jews. And he tried to restore the observance of the Sabbath and prevent mixed marriages. Eventually the wall was rebuilt.

∽

When Nehemiah, who might be fairly described as "a success", writes his memoirs, he ends, "Remember me with favour, my God" (Nehemiah

13 v 30). The word "favour" is the word "grace". "Show grace to me," he says. For all his many achievements Nehemiah hasn't brought the exile to an end—not in the way the prophets promised. The people are still breaking the Sabbath and still inter-marrying with pagans. At one point the people pray, "But see, we are slaves today, slaves in the land you gave our ancestors" (9 v 36). The people may be back in the land, but they're still under foreign rule. Nehemiah has not been able to address the underlying causes of the exile—human sin and divine judgment.

∽

Five centuries later the Jews were still under foreign rule, only this time it was Roman rule. They still longed for the exile to be over. They knew it wouldn't last for ever because, even before the exile had begun, Isaiah was prophesying its end: "Comfort, comfort my people, says your God" (Isaiah 40 v 1). He went on:

> *A voice of one calling:*
> *"In the wilderness prepare the way for the LORD;*
> *make straight in the desert a highway for our God." ...*
> *See, the Sovereign LORD comes with power ...*
> *He tends his flock like a shepherd:*
> *he gathers the lambs in his arms.*
>
> Isaiah 40 v 3, 10-11

Mark's Gospel omits the story of the birth of Jesus. Instead it cuts straight to John the Baptist. And Mark introduces him with this quote from Isaiah. John is the voice calling in the wilderness, preparing for the coming of the LORD. And if John is the voice in the wilderness, then Jesus must be the shepherd who gathers his flock. Jesus is the one who ends the exile. Jesus is the one who truly and completely leads us home.

But it's not the end of exile most Jews expected. What they have in mind is the defeat of the Romans and the restoration of Jewish autonomy—a return to a golden age with Jerusalem as the centre of the world. But Jesus had something much bigger and better in mind. He's going to tackle the root of the problem—human sin and divine judgment. He's going to lead us home to the presence of God in a restored Eden.

At the cross Jesus experienced exile from God. He died under darkness feeling abandoned by his Father. *"My God, my God, why have you forsaken me?"* he cried (Mark 15 v 34). He bore the judgment of sin that we deserve—a deep and profound exile from God. As a result he has opened the way for us to come home.

Maybe this Christmas you'll be going home. Coming home from a business trip in time for Christmas Day. Coming home after a term away at college. Coming home to your parents' house with all the security and familiarity which that involves. Maybe you will be busy preparing to welcome your children back home.

Let this homecoming be a reminder of the bigger and better homecoming that Jesus offers. Every time you pray, you are experiencing a mini-homecoming as you enter God's presence. But that's just a foretaste of the day when we come home to God's presence in a renewed Eden.

Meditate

He tends his flock like a shepherd:
he gathers the lambs in his arms.

(Isaiah 40 v 11)

O come, O come, Immanuel,
And ransom captive Israel,
That mourns in lonely exile here,
Until the Son of God appear.

O come, thou Rod of Jesse, free
Thine own from Satan's tyranny.
From depths of hell thy people save,
And give them victory o'er the grave.

(From the 12th-century Latin hymn, "O come, O come, Immanuel',
translation in Hymns Ancient and Modern)

Tim Chester

Prayer

I thank thee more that all our joy
is touched with pain,
That shadows fall on brightest hours,
that thorns remain;
So that earth's bliss may be our guide,
and not our chain.

I thank thee, Lord, that here our souls,
though amply blessed,
Can never find, although they seek,
a perfect rest;
Nor ever shall, until they lean
on Jesus' breast.
Amen.

(From "My God, I thank thee, who hast made" by Adelaide Procter)

The LORD

"The beginning of the good news about Jesus the Messiah, the Son of God, as it is written in Isaiah the prophet ... 'I will send my messenger ahead of you, who will prepare your way.'"

Mark 1 v 1-2

Storyline
Malachi 2 v 17 – 3 v 5 and Mark 11 – 13

If there is a God, why doesn't he use his power to put things right? Why doesn't he do something about war and poverty and oppression? God might be good or he might be all-powerful, but how can he be both? I'm sure you've been asked questions like these. You may have asked them yourself.

They're very contemporary questions. Only yesterday I was talking about Jesus to someone and they said, "But what about all the suffering in the world?" It's not a new question. People were asking questions like this back in the time of the prophet Malachi.

∽

We saw yesterday that Mark skips the nativity story and opens his Gospel with a quote from Isaiah. John the Baptist is the voice in the wilderness, heralding the one who will end the exile. But Mark doesn't just quote Isaiah. He also quotes the final book of the Old Testament, the prophet Malachi: "I will send my messenger ahead of you, who will prepare your way" (Mark 1 v 2).

Mark's point is that John the Baptist is the messenger promised by Malachi. But for whom is Malachi's promised messenger preparing? "You have wearied the LORD with your words," says Malachi. The people seem surprised. "How have we wearied him?" they ask (Malachi 2 v 17). Malachi's response is:

> *By saying, "All who do evil are good in the eyes of the LORD,*
> *and he is pleased with them" or "Where is the God of justice?"*
>
> Malachi 2 v 17

In other words their complaint is that God seems indifferent to evil. Indeed, evil people seem to prosper. Understandably, they, and we, ask, "If there is a God, why doesn't he use his power to put things right?" What's Malachi's response?

> *"I will send my messenger, who will prepare the way before*
> *me. Then suddenly the Lord you are seeking will come to his*
> *temple; the messenger of the covenant, whom you desire, will*
> *come," says the Lord Almighty.*   3 v 1

This is the extract that Mark's quotes. God *will* send a messenger, says Malachi, and then before you know what's happening, the LORD himself will come.

Then Malachi adds this darker postscript:

> *But who can endure the day of his coming? Who can stand*
> *when he appears? For he will be like a refiner's fire or a*
> *launderer's soap.*   3 v 2

Here's Malachi's point. You say you want God to do something about evil in the world. But don't you realise that you're evil? You'll be in the firing line along with everyone else. When the LORD comes in judgment, he'll come down your street. He'll knock on your door. That he delays is not a sign of his complacency. It's a sign of his patience.

But what is Mark's point when he quotes Malachi? Simply this: *that John is the forerunner and Jesus is the real thing.* Jesus is the Lord coming to his people. The Lord they seek is God himself and God himself will come in the person of Jesus. The baby in the manger, the boy from Nazareth, the man baptised with sinners in the Jordan is the Lord—as truly God as God can be.

∽

"The Lord you are seeking will come to his temple," says Malachi. And this is precisely what Jesus does in Mark 11 – 13. In a series of confrontations, Jesus condemns the religious system of the temple, just as he curses a fig tree in 11 v 12-23. He declares that not one stone of the temple will be left on another (13 v 2)—a judgment that came true when the Romans destroyed Jerusalem in AD 70.

But in Mark's Gospel there's a dramatic twist. The LORD *has* come in the person of Jesus. *But where's the judgment?* Jesus doesn't wrap up history. The final day of judgment doesn't come. The courtroom isn't convened.

But there is one act of judgment in Mark's Gospel. Judgment does indeed fall, but it falls on Jesus. He dies, cursed on a tree, under darkness, seemingly abandoned by God (15 v 33-37).

Jesus came first in grace as a substitute to die in our place. He bore the judgment we deserve so we can turn to him in faith and repentance and find hope. He died so that we need not fear his coming in judgment.

Because—make no mistake—he *will* come again. The period before Christmas is called "advent". The word means "coming" or "arrival". It's a time when Christians look forward to celebrating the coming of Jesus at Christmas. But it's also a time when Christians look forward to the second coming of Jesus; the moment when all mankind will face the final judgement of God.

∼

"If there's a God, why doesn't he do something about suffering?" asked my friend. The first answer is that God *has* already done something in the person of Jesus. Jesus came to die so we can be forgiven for the wrong we've done. The second answer is that God *will* do something. Jesus will come again to put right every wrong. In the meantime he gives us to the opportunity to repent. It is a mark of his great patience and mercy that he's delayed so long.

∼

Meditate
But who can endure the day of his coming?
Who can stand when he appears?

(Malachi 3 v 2)

Saints, before the altar bending,
Watching long in hope and fear,
Suddenly the Lord, descending,
In his temple shall appear.

Sinners, wrung with true repentance,
Doomed for guilt to endless pains,
Justice now revokes the sentence,
Mercy calls you—break your chains.

Come and worship, come and worship,
Worship Christ, the newborn King.

(From "Angels from the realms of glory" by James Montgomery)

∿

Prayer

Father God,
when we see the suffering of our world,
may we be angry because of the injustice others endure,
may we be repentant because of the wrong we commit,
may we be glad because of the salvation Jesus secures:
Jesus, who was born into suffering,
Jesus, who suffered to overcome suffering,
and Jesus, who rose again as the promise of
a world without suffering,
in whose name we pray.
Amen.

The One True Story

*"This is the genealogy of Jesus the Messiah
the son of David, the son of Abraham ...
Thus there were fourteen generations in all from
Abraham to David, fourteen from David to the exile to
Babylon, and fourteen from the exile to the Messiah."*
Matthew 1 v 1, 17

Storyline
Matthew 1 v 1-17

Imagine you hold in your hands a brand new copy of Matthew's Gospel. Perhaps you've received it as a Christmas present. It's hot off the press or, more accurately, the hand of the scribe who copied it is still aching from the effort. This is your first chance to read for yourself an eyewitness account of the life of the Jesus. What wonders will you read in its pages? In eager anticipation you turn to the first page and the opening words:

This is the genealogy of Jesus the Messiah the son of David, the son of Abraham:

*Abraham was the father of Isaac,
Isaac the father of Jacob,*

Jacob the father of Judah and his brothers…

Matthew 1 v 1-2

And so it goes on with a long list of names. Admittedly things pick up pretty quickly from verse 18 onwards. But the beginning is a bit of a disappointment. The No. 1 rule for writers is this: *open with a bang*. By that standard this book is a fail. Hands up who's started reading Matthew's Gospel and pretty quickly skipped to verse 18 or at least skimmed the first 17 verses. As I suspected—most of you.

∼

But instead of thinking of it as a rather dull list of generations, think of it as a list of rather exciting stories. We've met quite a few of these people already: Abraham on days 7 and 8, Isaac on days 7 and 18, Jacob on day 9, Jesse on day 15, David on days 15-18, Solomon on day 19, Ahaz on day 21, Hezekiah and Josiah on day 17. Some people in Matthew's list have been there in our readings without being name-checked. Others represent stories for which we haven't had space or which are now lost to the records of history. But all these stories have led to this, the most exciting and important story in human history: "the birth of Jesus the Messiah" (v 18).

Matthew's point is that the story of the Old Testament—and every story it contains—has come to a climax in the birth of this baby. Every story is a prelude to his story.

Or think of Matthew's genealogy as a series of hypertext links. Click on a name, and you'll be taken to an unfinished story that is left hanging… waiting for a final chapter. And Jesus is that final chapter.

Matthew picks out three key moments and highlights them by dividing his genealogy into groups of fourteen. In case you weren't counting, he spells it out in verse 17: "Thus there were fourteen generations in all from Abraham to David, fourteen from David to the exile to Babylon, and fourteen from the exile to the Messiah."

- ✎ The birth of Jesus fulfils *the promises to Abraham*.
- ✎ The birth of Jesus is *the birth of the son of David,* the eternal Saviour-King.
- ✎ The birth of Jesus signals *the end of exile* and our return home to God.

∼୨

It's not just Old Testament stories that find their fulfilment in Jesus. His story traces its origins back to the beginning of the world and beyond. He is the eternally begotten Son of God, the firstborn over creation, and the Wisdom through whom and for whom the world was made. Now at Christmas the Creator has entered his creation.

The storyteller has written himself into the script.

Nor is his story just the culmination of Israel's history. Jesus is the true image of God, the second Adam, the dragon-slayer, the true brother and the hope of all nations.

Matthew includes four women in his genealogy:

- ✎ v 3: Tamar pretended to be a prostitute (Genesis 38).
- ✎ v 5: Rahab was a Canaanite and a prostitute (Joshua 2).
- ✎ v 5: Ruth was from Moab (Ruth 1).
- ✎ v 6: Uriah's wife, Bathsheba, was the wife of a Hittite and committed adultery with King David (2 Samuel 11).

So all of them either had a shameful past or were Gentile or both. Yet here they are in the story and lineage of Jesus. They're here as a reminder that this story is for everyone—irrespective of our background or ethnicity.

And the story goes on. Matthew's Gospel ends with Jesus sending his followers out to disciple the nations. Somewhere along the line the story came to you. The fact that you hold this book in your hands is evidence of that fact.

And the story is still being written. The ending is clear—Jesus is coming again to restore all things. But in the meantime he invites you to find your identity as a character in his story. He invites you to make his story your story.

The story of Jesus is the one true story that makes sense of all our stories.

The key question for us is this: Do you want to hog the limelight? Do you want the applause of the audience? Do you want to steal every scene?

Or will you let Jesus be the lead while you rejoice in the privilege of being chosen to play a supporting role? Will you let him be the main character in your life? Will you let Jesus be the one true hero that he truly is?

∽

Meditate

The one and only Son ... has made him known.

(John 1 v 18)

O little town of Bethlehem,
How still we see thee lie.
Above thy deep and dreamless sleep
The silent stars go by.
Yet in thy dark streets shineth
The everlasting Light.

The hopes and fears of all the years
Are met in thee tonight.

(From "O little town of Bethlehem" by Phillips Brooks)

∾

Prayer

Lord Jesus Christ, you are the true Isaac,
the beloved Son of the Father, who was offered as a sacrifice,
but nevertheless did not succumb to the power of death.
And I entrust myself to you.

Lord Jesus Christ, you are the true Jacob,
the watchful shepherd, who has such great care for the
sheep which you guard.
And I entrust myself to you.

Lord Jesus Christ, you are the good and compassionate brother Joseph,
who in your glory is not ashamed to acknowledge his brothers,
however lowly and abject their condition.
And I entrust myself to you.
Lord Jesus Christ, you are the great sacrificer and bishop Melchizedek,
who has offered an eternal sacrifice once for all.
And I entrust myself to you.

Lord Jesus Christ, you are the sovereign lawgiver Moses,
writing your law on the tablets of our hearts by your Spirit.
And I entrust myself to you.

Lord Jesus Christ, you are the faithful captain and guide Joshua,
to lead us to the Promised Land.
And I entrust myself to you.

Lord Jesus Christ, you are my victorious and noble king David,
bringing by your hand all rebellious power to subjection.
And I entrust myself to you.

Lord Jesus Christ, you are my magnificent and triumphant king Solomon,
governing his kingdom in peace and prosperity.
And I entrust myself to you.

Lord Jesus Christ, you are my strong and powerful Samson,
who by his death has overwhelmed all his enemies.
And I entrust myself to you.

(Adapted from John Calvin, 1509-1564)

More from thegoodbook

Christmas playlist
Alastair Begg

A short, engaging, evangelistic book, perfect for giving away to non-Christian friends, family and church guests. Alastair Begg looks at the four songs sung at the original Christmas, and shows how they point to the real meaning of the season. Perfect for encouraging you, and for passing on to others.

ISBN (Paperback): 9781784981648
ISBN (Hardback): 9781784981662

How to have a happy Christmas
Tim Thornborough

You may love it or you may hate it, but one thing is certain. Christmas is coming, and you can't avoid it. Open, read and absorb this little booklet and we promise that you will have the happiest Christmas ever. Ideal for handing out to guests and church members at the conclusion of a Christmas service, or for delivering around your neighbourhood along with an invitation to your church services over Christmas.

ISBN: 9781784981617

A very different Christmas

**Rico Tice and
Nate Morgan Locke**

An intriguingly different introduction to Christianity which invites readers to open Christmas gifts from the Father, Son and Holy Spirit. Ideal for giving away in the holiday season. Buy it, read it, give it away!

ISBN: 9781784980146

5 things to pray for the people you love
Rachel Jones
ISBN: 9781910307397

5 things to pray for your church
Rachel Jones
ISBN: 9781784980306

Two books of practical help and encouragement that are crammed with ideas and fresh Bible perspectives to breathe new life into your prayers.

thegoodbook.com | .co.uk | .com.au | .co.nz

More from 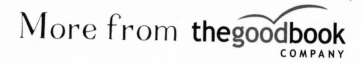 thegoodbook COMPANY

Explore with the Reformers
90 days with Calvin, Luther, Bullinger and Cranmer

Let Calvin, Luther, Bullinger and Cranmer sit alongside you as you open up your Bible day by day.

The writings of these Reformers have been edited, and in parts translated, by Dr Lee Gatiss. Each day includes helpful questions and prompts to apply the Reformers' insights to your life.

2017 is the 500th anniversary of the Reformation. Bring it to life in your own devotional walk with God.

Explore with the Reformers includes brief biographies of John Calvin, Martin Luther, Heinrich Bullinger and Thomas Cranmer.

Enjoy the treasures of Genesis, the Psalms, Galatians, the Ten Commandments, and more.

ISBN: 9781784980863

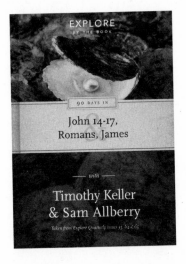

90 Days in John 14-17, Romans, James
Timothy Keller and Sam Allberry

90 days of open-Bible devotionals with Timothy Keller and Sam Allberry. Includes space for journaling.

ISBN: 9781784981228

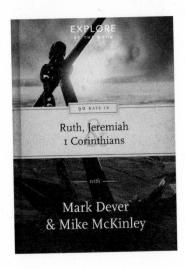

90 Days in Ruth, Jeremiah and 1 Corinthians
Mark Dever and Mike McKinley

90 days of open-Bible devotionals with Mark Dever and Mike McKinley. Includes space for journaling.

ISBN: 9781784981235

More from thegoodbook COMPANY

Explore Daily Devotional

These short studies help you open up the Scriptures regularly, and will encourage and equip you in your walk with God. *Explore* is available as a printed book of dated notes published four times a year, or as an app. It features careful Bible engagement with insightful application, and is written by trusted Bible teachers including Tim Keller, Mark Dever, Tim Chester, David Helm and Ray Ortlund.

thegoodbook.com | .co.uk | .com.au | .co.nz

thegoodbook

COMPANY

Opening up the Bible

At The Good Book Company, we are dedicated to helping Christians and local churches grow. We believe that God's growth process always starts with hearing clearly what He has said to us through His timeless word—the Bible.

Ever since we opened our doors in 1991, we have been striving to produce resources that honour God in the way the Bible is used. We have grown to become an international provider of user-friendly resources to the Christian community, with believers of all backgrounds and denominations using our Bible studies, books, evangelistic resources, DVD-based courses and training events.

We want to equip ordinary Christians to live for Christ day by day, and churches to grow in their knowledge of God, their love for one another, and the effectiveness of their outreach.

Call us for a discussion of your needs or visit one of our local websites for more information on the resources and services we provide.

Your friends at The Good Book Company

UK & EUROPE
NORTH AMERICA
AUSTRALIA
NEW ZEALAND

thegoodbook.co.uk
thegoodbook.com
thegoodbook.com.au
thegoodbook.co.nz

0333 123 0880
866 244 2165
(02) 9564 3555
(+64) 3 343 2463

WWW.CHRISTIANITYEXPLORED.ORG
Our partner site is a great place for those exploring the Christian faith, with a clear explanation of the good news, powerful testimonies and answers to difficult questions.